ALI

MUHAMMAD

MUHAMMAD ALI TAKES A STROLL THROUGH LONDON PRIOR TO HIS FIRST FIGHT WITH ENGLAND'S HENRY COOPER IN 1963.

To my sons Jay and Joel, who try to understand my passion for boxing, and to Mack Lewis, my guru.

10 9 8 7 6 5 4 3 2 1

Text and design copyright © Carlton Books Limited, 2000

MetroBooks

An Imprint of Friedman/Fairfax Publications

This edition published by Metrobooks by arrangement with Carlton Books Limited.

ISBN 1 58663 033 4

Project Editor: Chris Hawkes
Project Art Direction: Brian Flynn
Production: Bob Bhamra
Picture Research: Catherine Costelloe

Printed and bound in Italy

MUHAMMAD ALI

The Eye-Witness Story of a Boxing Legend

Alan Goldstein

MetroBooks

Contents

Foreword by George Foreman

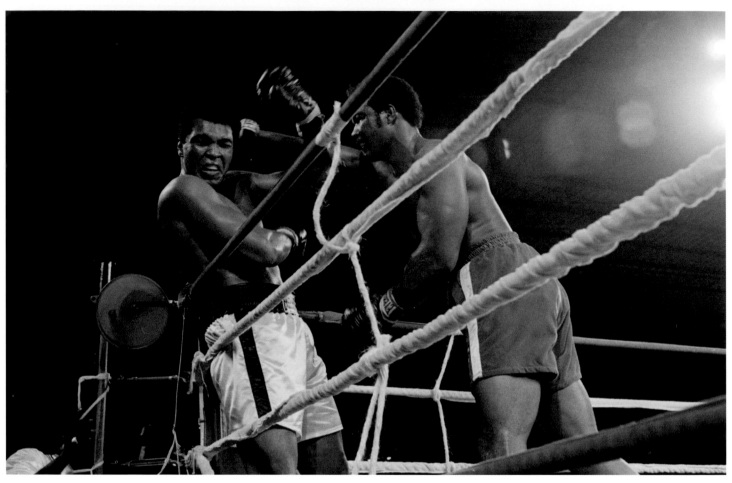

ACTION FROM A MEMORABLE NIGHT IN KINSHASA, ZAIRE.

Mention me and Muhammad Ali in the same breath and people immediately think about our championship fight in Zaire in 1974 that became known as "The Rumble in the Jungle". Of course, that was when Ali first used his "Rope-A-Dope" tactics. I punched myself into exhaustion and lost my heavyweight crown.

It took me a long, long time to put that behind me. I tried to convince myself and anyone who might listen that I'd been victimized by a set of circumstances beyond my control. And, for years, I admit I hated Ali. But as I grew older and wiser, I was able to reconcile that defeat and acknowledge that he beat me fair and square.

I wanted a rematch in the worst way, but the result could have easily been the same. In the end, I realized I had lost to a great champion who transcended the sport of boxing, and that I should be proud to have been a big chapter in his legendary career.

It's difficult to explain, but Muhammad has remained a strong presence in my life. I used to wake up nights in a sweat thinking about that fight in Africa. I know it was the turning point in my life. It taught me humility. When they raised his hand in victory, I finally realized I wasn't powerful enough to control everything, that there was something bigger than me. It led me to God and I eventually became a spokesman for Jesus Christ.

Sometimes, I almost feel like a father to him. I wish we had gotten to know each other better over the years, gone fishing, or just spent time talking about life. Now, I can only pray for Muhammad in his battle with Parkinson's syndrome. He has handled the fight with great dignity.

But we did have some good times together. We shared a stage in Los Angeles when they were honoring former Olympic champions before the 1984 Games. We were having a religious debate when it came time for Ali to speak. I noticed his shirt-tail was hanging out of his pants. I reached over and tucked it in. That was the least I could do for the man who had taught me so much about how to carry myself in and out of the ring. In my heart, he will always be "The Greatest".

Introduction

For the past four decades, Muhammad Ali, a.k.a. Cassius Clay, has cast a giant shadow over the world of sports.

He first became a worldwide figure in 1960 by winning a gold medal in the Rome Olympics as a virile, gifted light-heavyweight. Thirty-six years later in Atlanta, his body ravaged by Parkinson's syndrome, Ali touched everyone's heart as he valiantly made his tortuous, slow journey up a flight of stairs to light the Olympic torch.

In the years between, he managed to affect the lives of people in every corner of the world. Arguably, he was the first truly global athlete, staging championship bouts in such Third World sites as Djakarta, Kinshasa and Kuala Lumpur.

The lord of the ring and three-time heavyweight champion was always more than a mere prize fighter. He would lose his title on the canvas and in the legal courts fighting for the right to practice his adopted Muslim religion. But in or out of the ring, he always managed to steal the spotlight.

A theater critic once suggested Ali was an actor playing the part of an athlete, and Ali, the entertainer, was as important as the heavyweight king who transcended the blood sport of boxing.

ALI WAVES TO ADORING FANS BEFORE HIS FIRST FIGHT WITH HENRY COOPER IN LONDON.

ALI PREDICTED A FIFTH-ROUND KNOCK-OUT OF COOPER AND KEPT HIS WORD.

He would assume so many roles that, at times, it seemed even Ali forgot which part he was currently playing—clown, prophet, poet, preacher, anti-Establishment advocate or international ambassador of peace. Part fact, part myth. In retrospect, he was aptly described as the jester of President Kennedy's Camelot years and the suffering saint of the Vietnam era.

In the 1960s he was the most recognizable face on earth, first for his stunning upset of the seemingly invincible Sonny Liston and later as a symbol of America's rage for refusing induction into the Army during the height of the Vietnam War. The general populace was not ready to embrace a brash black man who was the first athletic superstar to adopt the Muslim faith and discard his "slave name". At the same time, his anti-Establishment stand, which resulted in a three-year exile from the ring, made him the ultimate expression of Black Power.

Ali returned to center stage in 1970, resuming his boxing career and winning classic battles against Joe Frazier, George Foreman and Earnie Shavers. Like so many boxing legends before him, he competed far too long, leading to embarrassing and painful beatings by Larry Holmes and Trevor Berbick before finally quitting.

As a sportswriter whose journalistic career coincided with Ali's, we had the good fortune of covering many of his major fights, but remember him more for his ever-changing personality.

He could tickle your funny bone spouting doggerel or performing magic tricks, but also send a shudder up your spine the way he tortured Floyd Patterson and Ernie Terrell who both refused to acknowledge Ali's transformation to the nation of Islam. But we could also recall uncommon acts of kindness when he made impromptu visits to hospitals to encourage cancer patients or when he gave a sizeable donation to save a Jewish home for the aged from bankruptcy.

In recent years, his unquestionable spirit in battling his disease and his religious devotion has made him a public icon. Forgotten are the days of yore when his braggadocio manner polarized fight fans. But such a time also provided our most enduring memory of Ali displaying his inspired inventiveness.

After concluding a public sparring session in preparation for his match with Shavers in Madison Square Garden in 1977, Ali engaged in his all-too-familiar "Float like a butterfly, sting like a bee" duet with straight man Bundini Brown. Finally, he strolled to a corner and bellowed down a hollow ring post, "The Greatest of All Time." And the boast then reverberated throughout the vast arena. In retrospect, who could argue the point?

ONE

The Early Years

How many great journeys in life *have begun* on a shiny new bicycle?

As mythology tells us, **it did for 12-year-old**

Cassius Clay, who, quite by accident,

or fate, *as many would later suggest,*

found his serendipity way to a boxing gym

in downtown Louisville

Ali tended to side with the fatalists. He told biographer Thomas Hauser, "I don't know what it was, but I always felt like I was born to do something for my people. When I was 8 or 10, I'd walk out of my house at two in the morning and look to the sky for an angel or revelation or God telling me what to do.

"I'd look at the stars, wait for a voice, but I never heard nothing. Then my bike got stolen and I started boxing. It was like God was telling me I had a responsibility." [1]

But going to the gym had not been his intention. He had joined a friend in a visit to the annual Home Show, an event where the city's black merchants showed their wares and tempted the public with the promise of free food and drink. It was an offer young Cassius, who had to rely on his mother's inventiveness to fill his dinner plate, could not refuse.

After a night of gluttony, he discovered his $60 bicycle was missing. Tears gained the attention of sympathetic adults who directed him to the building's basement where a white policeman, Joe Martin, spent his off-duty hours training amateur boxers.

Cassius informed Martin of his plight and vowed to catch and whip the thief. Martin assessed the spindly 80-pound youth and suggested learning how to fight before seeking revenge.

In retrospect, it would be easy imagining the novice tyro becoming an instant success

CASSIUS CLAY STRIKES A FIGHTING POSE BEFORE HIS AMATEUR DEBUT.

at the "sweet science" of boxing, but his natural ability was neither apparent to Martin nor Cassius, who pictured himself "fighting like a girl, throwing wild, looping punches". [2]

But the burning ambition to separate himself from the crowd was already evident. On his first day in the gym he challenged a seasoned fighter and suffered a bloody nose and mouth for his troubles.

As Martin later recalled, "If amateur boxers were paid bonuses like baseball players, I don't think Cassius would have received one. He was just ordinary the first year. But a year later, you could see that this little smart aleck had potential. He stood out because he had more determination than most boys, and he had the speed to get him someplace. He was a kid willing to make the sacrifices necessary to achieve something worthwhile in sports, and I recognized it was almost impossible to discourage him." [3]

Nothing would ever discourage young Cassius, who, after only a few winning appearances on Martin's sponsored television show, *Tomorrow's Champions*, informed his parents he would one day be champion of the world.

This seemed his destiny from the day his mother nicknamed him "GG", on account of the first sounds he uttered as a baby. Later, a mature Muhammad Ali would joke, "I was actually

SURROUNDED BY HIS PARENTS AND SIX MEMBERS OF A LOUISVILLE-BASED SYNDICATE, CLAY SIGNS HIS FIRST PROFESSIONAL CONTRACT.

trying to say 'Golden Gloves'," [4]—his first stepping stone to winning four Kentucky state crowns and two National AAU titles as a prelude to his 1960 Olympic triumph in Rome.

Several noted amateur officials saw greatness in him almost immediately. "Even as an amateur, he had the same reflexes and skills he had later on," said chief AAU referee Bob Surkein. "Usually you see amateurs jump out of harm's way. But Cassius would stand there and just move his head six inches and his body six inches and slide away. I knew this kid had it." [5]

Surkein also recalled staying at the same hotel as Cassius during a tournament. Seeking to follow the results in the local newspaper, he discovered 16 copies were minus the sports section. A trip to Cassius's room quickly solved the mystery. He discovered the impressionable fighter cutting out his picture from every edition.

By now, Cassius was already declaring himself "The Greatest". It has been written he borrowed the phrase from flamboyant wrestler Gorgeous George, but it was just as likely he copied it from his father, Cassius Marcellus Clay Sr., who enjoyed performing as a singer and dancer in the neighborhood between jobs as a house and sign painter.

Historians would debate whether Muhammad Ali was the product of a dirt-poor or middle-class environment so passionately that author Wilfred Sheed caustically wrote, "it would be different from day to day like alternate street parking." [6]

Ali remembered there seldom being enough food to feed him and his younger brother Rudolph (a.k.a Rahaman). His mother, Odessa, helped compensate for her husband's irregular paycheck by working as a domestic in white neighborhoods for $4 a day. The boys usually wore clothes purchased from the Good Will store and shoes with cardboard inserts.

Louisville police records reveal that his father, who had trouble maintaining his temper after a drinking bout, threatened his wife on several occasions—traumatic incidents Ali chose to forget in his memoirs. As one pseudo-psychologist suggested, "You find great men to have loved their mothers but imitated their fathers." [7]

There were no apparent psychological scars left on Ali from his family life, only deep-hearted bitterness over the segregation policies of the South. Despite his early notoriety, he still heard chants of "Nigger" whenever venturing out of the ghetto and quickly learned he was unwelcome in downtown hotels, restaurants and theaters.

His mother remembered an adolescent Cassius looking in the storefront of offices and wondering aloud, "Where are all the colored folk?" [8]

His designated status as a "second-class citizen" would serve as a far greater motivating force more than his natural ambition to achieve a measure of success. It would drive him to become an Olympic gold medalist, thrice world heavyweight champion, and, in the Sixties, the most recognized face in the universe.

A GOLDEN GLOVES CHAMPION, YOUNG CASSIUS SETS HIS SIGHTS ON THE 1960 OLYMPICS.

"He didn't know a left hook from a kick in the butt. But he was the most dedicated fighter I ever saw. He lived in the gym. He was there when I arrived in the morning and he was there when I left at night."

Amateur trainer **JOE MARTIN**, on Clay's first days in gym. (*Louisville Courier-Journal*, 9.15.1978)

A Golden Start

It was the summer of 1960 and Cassius Clay was enjoying

a break from training at Fort Dix, N.J., with the United States

Olympic boxing team. He decided to join amateur

official Bob Surkein on a visit to Atlantic City. Pausing

on the famous boardwalk, he asked innocently,

"What do you think is across this big lake?"

"His geography wasn't too good," said Surkein,

"but he had his mind on Rome for a long time."

A STRONG RALLY IN THE FINAL AGAINST POLAND'S PIETRZKOWSKI GAVE CASSIUS THE GOLD MEDAL.

Indeed. A lean and hungry Cassius was thinking of the glory of Rome from the days he first began bringing home medals and trophies to his modest home in Louisville. As the spoils of victory quickly overflowed the shelves, his confidence and ambition started to grow exponentially.

He had already tested his mettle against a number of pros. On one of his first encounters with future trainer Angelo Dundee, he badgered Dundee into letting him spar with Willie Pastrano, who was on his way to winning the light-heavyweight crown.

Dundee, who frowned on the idea of amateurs working with pros, finally agreed. After three minutes of watching the teenage Cassius use Pastrano's face like a speed bag, Dundee shouted "Enough! Willie's got a big fight coming up." [2]

True, there were a few minor pitfalls on the way to Rome. Clay lost in the 1959 Pan-American Games Trials to lefthanded Amos Johnson, a mature fighter representing the Marines. He accepted the loss philosophically. "I just couldn't figure him out," he said. [3]

But he already had his eye on the biggest prize. In high school, a day-dreaming Clay would adorn the back of his jacket with bold lettering that read "Heavyweight Champion of the World".

Middleweight Skeeter McClure, who became fast friends with Clay as they joined in dominating the pre-Olympic competition, soon realized the young Kentucky boxer was unique.

"The first time I saw him," McClure told *GQ* magazine, "his pants were too short and his arms were too long for his sleeves. Even then he fought in an unorthodox way. He kept his hands down and threw only head punches. But he had great legs and great speed. To see a heavyweight move like that was really something.

"The next year we both made the team and went to Rome. One day, between bouts, he told me, 'I've got 11 millionaires back in Louisville who are going to put up money for me. I'm going to make them rich and I'm going to be rich, and I'm going to become heavyweight

CASSIUS CLAY STANDS PROUDLY ON THE VICTORY STAND DISPLAYING HIS GOLD
MEDAL AS 178-POUND OLYMPIC GAMES CHAMPION IN ROME.

champion of the world.' I said 'Yeah, right.' In those days no one was putting that kind of money in a fighter's kitty … One day after the Olympics, I was sitting at home eating breakfast. I opened the paper and there he was, Cassius Clay, with a roomful of millionaires." [4]

Negotiations had already started in anticipation of Cassius winning the gold in the 178-pound division, a feat he would accomplish by beating Zbigniew Pietrzykowski of Poland, a three-time European champion and bronze medalist in the 1956 Olympics.

Pietrzykowski's southpaw style confused Cassius in the opening round and the bell for the second round still saw the American trailing on the judges' cards.

But the final round was a tour de force for the young Clay. As English journalist John

Cottrell wrote, "In the final round he finally found his form, moving in and out with expert judgment, punching crisply and with perfect timing. This sharper, better-coordinated Clay stormed back with a torrent of combination punching that left Pietrzykowksi dazed. At the final bell the Pole was slumped helplessly on the ropes. There was no doubting the verdict." [5]

Clay arrived home to a triumphant welcome. A motorcade carried the 18-year-old Olympic champion and his family to a celebration at his high school. One news story called the gold medal "the biggest prize a black boy has brought back to Louisville". The gold medal, as folklore would have it, ultimately found its way to the bottom of the Ohio River, the result of young Cassius's frustration with the continued bigotry displayed in his home town. Soon after his return, he was refused service at a hamburger joint. The story of the discarded prize is now considered apocryphal, but medals would soon be replaced by hard currency.

Cassius's father had already rejected the entreaties of Joe Martin, a policeman who was his son's original trainer and acting as a courier for tobacco millionaire, William Reynolds. Historians would claim Clay Sr.'s, decision was based on his hatred of white policemen, but his son was more repelled by Reynolds's attitude. He felt he had been treated no better than a slave during a summer of working at the millionaire's Louisville estate.

Instead, he turned to a group of 11 white men—ten of them millionaires representing most of the wealth in Kentucky. William Faversham, who made his fortune in whiskey, would head the group. Clay received a $10,000 signing bonus and a guaranteed $4,000 against future earnings for the first two years. All purses would be split in half the first four years and 60–40 thereafter.

It was hardly a King's ransom and not worthy of the posed photo on the cover of *Sports Illustrated* depicting a wide-mouthed Cassius Clay seated in a bank vault atop a mountain of one million dollar bills. The caption read: "I'll take my million and run." In truth, it was just a small down payment on an unparalleled career.

RETURNING FROM ROME, CASSIUS GETS A KISS FROM HIS MOTHER, ODESSA, WHILE HIS FATHER, CASSIUS SR, AND BROTHER, RUDY, LOOK ON.

TWO

The Early Fights

Ode To An Old Man

It was that night at the Coliseum that I annihilated him
I gave him a lot of sand
The one they call the old man.
I swept that old man clean out of the ring
'Cause a brand new broom will clean up most anything.
He was trying to remain the Great Mr Moore
But Cassius said: *"He must go in four!"*

CASSIUS CLAY, 1962 [1]

True to his prediction, Clay had left the baldheaded Moore, 40, but looking more like 80, flat on his back in the fourth round of their heralded dust-up at the Los Angeles Sports Arena. At least one person in the crowd of over 16,000 was made a believer of Cassius' divine powers. As Clay recalled, "This middle-aged man, with a wild look in his eyes, grabbed me by the arm and asked 'Are you God?' I said, 'No sir, I'm Cassius Clay, the Greatest.'" [2]

It had been a classic revival of an all-too-familiar script—a rising star taking advantage of a once-great fighter twice his age. In fact Clay, after first being rebuffed by his ring idol, Ray Robinson, had sought out Moore as a mentor before turning professional.

At the time, the crafty, old "Mongoose" was still the reigning light heavyweight champion. Realizing he was well past his prime, Moore regarded the precocious Clay as the golden goose who had found the secret formula to making a fortune in boxing through his braggadocio and uncanny ability to make his prophecies ring true.

Beginning with Willi Besmanoff in his tenth pro fight, Ali had become the Nostradamus of pugilism by successfully predicting the round he would finish his foe in seven of eight bouts.

In their brief alliance at Moore's rudimentary training camp in San Diego, aptly nick-named "The Salt Mines" where Cassius had to function as a dishwasher after completing his boxing regimen, Archie tried to convince Clay to abandon his flitting style in favor of a power game that would guarantee longevity. Clay balked at the offer.

"I don't want to fight until I'm an old man," he said. "I'm gonna only fight five or six years, make $2 or $3 million and quit fighting." [3]

Of course, like so many boxing legends, he would continue to fight long after his skills had eroded. But in his youth, Clay boasted the speed and resourcefulness to overcome the absence of basic fundamentals.

His early conquests against the likes of Tunney Hunsaker, Herb Siler, Tony Esperti and Jim Robinson were hardly noteworthy. And his ten round decision over the rugged Duke Sabedong is remembered more for his pre-fight encounter with Gorgeous George, who was appearing in Las Vegas a few days earlier. The flamboyant wrestler's shtick made a profound impact on the impressionable Clay. Said Cassius, "I'd never been shy about talking, but I decided then that if I talked even more, there was no telling how much money people would pay to see me." [4]

Despite his self-proclaimed invincibility, Clay soon proved he was quite human. Making his pro debut at Madison Square Garden on February 10, 1962, he suffered a minor embarrassment. He had predicted a fourth-round knockout of Sonny Banks, who was considered a decent puncher. Before the fight, he let his guard down momentarily, asking cornerman Gil Clancy, "Do you think I can beat this guy?" [5]

His self-doubt increased in the first round when Banks dropped him with a left hook. But the shocking impact of hitting the canvas quickly revived him, and Clay went on to finish Banks in the appointed round. It convinced head trainer Angelo Dundee that his protégé had the courage and conviction to go with his natural gifts.

The fight with Doug Jones in New York 13 months later would be a better measuring stick in a number of ways. First, it tested Clay's ingenuity as a self-promoter in the face of a city-wide newspaper strike. He was forced to match his iambic pentameter against a group of female, beatnik poets in Greenwich Village. Declaring it "no contest", Cassius said, "The rhythm of my poetry gives me an unprecedented rhythm in the ring." [6]

But he was definitely out of step against Jones who was dancing to a different beat. A man on a mission, Jones refused to chase his jiving rival, preferring to stand his ground in mid-ring while flurrying on occasion. The strategy worked well enough to leave the fight's outcome in doubt. Two scorecards gave Clay a one-round margin, but the 8-1-1 vote of the third judge was an early indication of how Clay's legerdemain could mesmerize a jury.

The capacity crowd, remembering Clay's prediction of a fourth-round knockout, loudly booed the verdict and was quick to label him a false prophet. Critics renewed their old complaints. Columnist Arthur Daley of the *New York Times* wrote, "The exceedingly likeable Clay is lousing up his public relations by his boasting, and it's hard time he eased off." [7]

Such warnings hardly affected Clay whose mouth was in full throttle prior to his next match in London against popular British champion Henry Cooper, whom he labeled "a bum".

"Our 'Enery" was a gallant warrior who had to overcome the handicap of a battle-scarred face that would spurt blood at the slightest provocation. That was to be the scenario through the first three rounds when Clay shredded the plodding Brit's features with his rapier jab.

Having predicted Cooper would fall in the fifth, Cassius mugged and preened in the fourth round, even pausing to cast an eye in the direction of Elizabeth Taylor who was screaming for referee Tommy Little to end the slaughter. In that brief moment, Cooper launched a desperate left hook that landed flush on his tormentor's chin. Clay fell through the ropes, but managed to clamber back on rubbery legs to be saved by the bell.

It was now time for Dundee to work his own brand of magic. In the first round, he had noticed an open seam in one of Clay's gloves. Now, in a time of crisis, he deftly widened the tear, gesturing to the referee and gaining valuable time for his stunned fighter to recuperate.

When the battle resumed, Clay was quickly back in command and finished the job in the fifth round as promised. Waiting in the dressing room was Jack Nilon, heavyweight champion Sonny Liston's co-manager. "I've flown 3,000 miles just to tell you Liston wants you," he said. "Sonny wants you to stay healthy. You've talked yourself into a title fight. Now your wife can be a rich widow." [8]

Cassius responded with a roar of approval. He had made his prediction seven months earlier after whipping Archie Moore. That night the blackboard in his dressing room was emblazoned with the message: "Liston in Eight—Next Champ, Cassius."

HUNSAKER

vs. Tunney Hunsaker
October 29, 1960

FREEDOM HALL, LOUISVILLE, KENTUCKY. WON 6.

IT WAS TARGET PRACTICE FOR CASSIUS CLAY AGAINST TUNNEY HUNSAKER IN HIS SUCCESSFUL SIX-ROUND PRO DEBUT.

"I'd had some 40-odd fights and knew some tricks, and, believe me, I tried them all on Ali that night. I know I made him a little upset, but nothing could match his speed as a heavyweight, and he attacked you from a hundred different angles ... I lost,

but I still treasure the memory
because to me, *he really was* 'The Greatest'."

TUNNEY HUNSAKER, (*Baltimore Sun*, 1.17.1992)

vs. Herb Siler
December 27, 1960

AUDITORIUM, MIAMI BEACH, FLORIDA. KO4.

"I think I was paid $80 for fighting Clay. They offered me that because they were trying to bring him along and they thought I was a spoiler. **I think the people who had money invested in Clay were afraid I would do something drastic and hurt him.** It was stopped in the fourth on a TKO because I had a heavy cut in the mouth, but he never hurt me."

HERB SILER, (*Sports Illustrated*, 9.29.1980)

vs. Tony Esperti
January 17, 1961

AUDITORIUM, MIAMI BEACH, FLORIDA. KO3.

"I just came out of jail for unlawful entry and fought Ali when I was 28. I was working out at the Fifth Street Gym in Miami and Chris Dundee asked me if I wanted to fight a kid named Cassius Clay. I was broke, so I said O.K. "At the time I fought him, **I knew he could box, but I didn't think he had much heart.**

I met him later in the Dade County jail. He was getting harassed and they put him in there for five days on a traffic violation. When he saw me, he said, 'That's my man. How long have you been here?'"

TONY ESPERTI, (*Sports Illustrated*, 9.29.1980)

CASSIUS DISPLAYS A STREAMLINED PHYSIQUE IN HIS EARLY DAYS AS A PROFESSIONAL WHEN HE DAZZLED RIVALS WITH HIS HAND AND FOOT SPEED.

vs. Jim Robinson
January 7, 1961

CONVENTION HALL, MIAMI BEACH, FLORIDA. KO1.

"I'd read about Clay, and my manager asked me if I wanted to fight him.
I said I couldn't, 'cause I weighed only 158 pounds.
He said, *'We'll work something out.'* At the weigh-in,
he took my finger and pressed down until the scale registered 178 pounds.

"In the first round, he bloodied my nose. But I was a smart fighter. I'd been fighting before he was born.

But he caught me with a right hand. I sat on my knee and took a nine count before getting up.

The referee looked at my nose and stopped it."

JIM ROBINSON, (*Sports Illustrated*, 9.29.1980)

vs. Donny Fleeman
February 21, 1961

CONVENTION HALL, MIAMI BEACH, FLORIDA. KO1.

"I had fought Pete Rademacher a few weeks earlier in Washington, and he cracked my ribs and damaged my spleen.

Clay was going to be one of my last fights anyway.
I had 47 fights, but never took fighting seriously.
There was no money to be made.
For Clay, I got a guarantee of $3,000.

I remember he was real fast and he hit me where it hurt the most. It seemed he was well-connected and knew just where

I was having trouble. "I'd have to say, even in politics, he proved himself. **On Vietnam, he had a point and he stood up for it.**

Maybe, at the time, I didn't think he was right, but times change, and he turned out to be right. **He was a brave man."**

DONNY FLEEMAN, (*Sports Illustrated*, 9.29.1980)

STILL ONLY 21, CASSIUS CLAY WAS ALREADY AS BRASH AS A CHAMPION IN PREDICTING THE QUICK DOWNFALL OF LAMAR CLARK IN THEIR FIGHT IN KENTUCKY.

CLARK
vs. Lamar Clark
April 19, 1961

FREEDOM HALL, LOUISVILLE, KENTUCKY. KO2.

"I first met him at the weigh-in and he was as cocky as he is now.

He made up a poem about me and called me the *'Utah farmer'*.

Ali said before the fight he was going to retire me and, in fact, it was my last fight. It only lasted two rounds. He caught me with a

left and right and broke my nose. There were tears in my eyes. When he came to see me after the fight,

he apologized for hurting me." **LAMAR CLARK,** (*Sports Illustrated*, 9.29.1980)

SABEDONG

vs. Duke Sabedong
June 26, 1961

CONVENTION CENTER, LAS VEGAS, NEVADA. WON 10.

"He kept saying, **'The big guy will go in four.'**
I was 6' 7" and when he saw me,
he looked at Angelo Dundee as if to say,
'What do I do with this guy?'

"I had trouble hitting him; he was very fast. The first time I hit him low,
his eyes got as big as saucers. I was also going to bite his ear.
I don't think Ali was the greatest I fought."

DUKE SABEDONG, (*Sports Illustrated*, 9.29.1980)

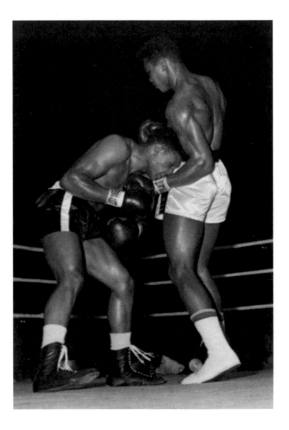

JOHNSON

vs. Alonzo Johnson
July 22, 1961

FREEDOM HALL, LOUISVILLE, KENTUCKY. WON 10.

CLAY WAS FORCED TO GO TEN ROUNDS IN HIS
SECOND STRAIGHT FIGHT BEFORE GETTING
THE NOD OVER ALONZO JOHNSON.

MITEFF
vs. Alex Miteff
October 7, 1961

FREEDOM HALL, LOUISVILLE, KENTUCKY. KO6.

"He was no puncher, didn't punch hard at all. But he had me on the canvas in the sixth round. The referee stopped it. I think back now and say to myself *I have known two very great men,* the ex-President of my country, **Juan Peron,** and **Muhammad Ali.**"

ALEX MITEFF, (*Sports Illustrated*, 9.29.1980)

A RIGHT HAND BY CLAY ROCKS ALEX MITEFF BEFORE HE STOPPED HIS ARGENTINE RIVAL IN THE SIXTH ROUND.

vs. Willi Besmanoff
November 29, 1961

FREEDOM HALL, LOUISVILLE, KENTUCKY. KO7.

"I'm embarrassed to get in the ring with this unrated duck.
I'm ready for top contenders."

CASSIUS CLAY on Willi Besmanoff. (Jose Torres, *Sting Like A Bee*, p.118)

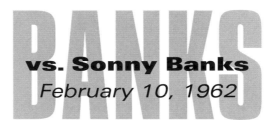

vs. Sonny Banks
February 10, 1962

MADISON SQUARE GARDEN, NEW YORK CITY. KO4.

"Banks hit him right on the jaw in the first round, and on the way down, his eyes were closed.
But when his butt hit the floor, he woke up.
That's when I saw his recuperative powers."

Trainer, ANGELO DUNDEE, on Clay getting dropped for the first time as a pro by Sonny Banks.

(Thomas Hauser, *Muhammad Ali: His Life and Times*, p.43)

WARNER

vs. Don Warner
February 28, 1962

CONVENTION HALL, MIAMI BEACH, FLORIDA. KO4.

DON WARNER TAKES COVER DURING A BARRAGE BY CLAY, WHO SCORED A FOURTH-ROUND KNOCK-OUT.

vs. George Logan
April 23, 1962

MEMORIAL SPORTS ARENA, LOS ANGELES. KO4.

"If Ali had gone to fight for his country, there would be no question, no doubt, that he was the greatest." GEORGE LOGAN, (*Sports Illustrated*, 9.29.1980)

vs. Billy Daniels
May 19, 1962

ST. NICHOLAS ARENA, NEW YORK CITY. KO7.

"Clay won the first two rounds. In the second, he gave me a bad cut. I was having trouble hitting him with a straight right, so I started looping my punches. **In the fifth, I hurt him.** That's when I made a serious mistake. I didn't press my advantage because I thought it was wise to pace myself. He tired in the seventh and I figured I had him. Then the referee called the whole thing off, **but Cassius never hurt me.**"

BILLIE DANIELS, *New York World Telegram,* date unavailable.

vs. Alejandro Lavorante
July 20, 1962

MEMORIAL SPORTS ARENA, LOS ANGELES. KO5.

"Cassius looked like a million bucks in stopping Lavorante in five. We figured he was ready to fight Archie Moore."

ANGELO DUNDEE, (Thomas Hauser, *Muhammad Ali, His Life and Times.*)

vs. Archie Moore
November 15, 1962

MEMORIAL SPORTS ARENA, LOS ANGELES. KO4.

"I'm tired of telling you I'm the greatest. From now on, I'll let you say it.

I would have beaten Archie Moore if he was still

in his 20s. I am here to resurrect the fight game.

I've had 15 fights, won 13 by knockouts and

this was the 12th time I called the round.

I think I have enough ability to call the round

against anybody I fight."

CASSIUS CLAY to media after successfully fulfilling his fourth-round
KO prediction against Archie Moore on November 15, 1962.
(*Boxing Illustrated*, February, 1963)

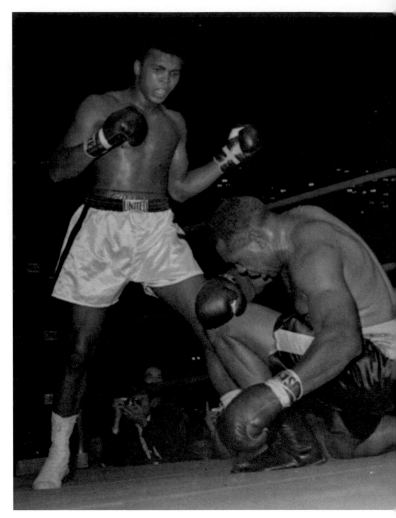

TRUE TO HIS PREDICTION, CLAY DISPOSED OF ARCHIE MOORE IN FOUR ROUNDS.

vs. Charlie Powell
January 24, 1963

CIVIC ARENA, PITTSBURGH, PENNSYLVANIA. KO3.

"When he first hit me, I thought to myself,
I can take two of those to get in one of my own.
But in a little while, I found out I was getting dizzier
and dizzier every time he hit me.
**Clay throws punches so easily you don't realize how
much they shock you until it is too late.**"

CHARLIE POWELL, (*Sports Illustrated*, 2.24.64)

vs. Doug Jones
March 13, 1963

MADISON SQUARE GARDEN, NEW YORK CITY. WON 10.

"The referee was most accurate.
See, **I'm pretty as a girl.** There isn't a mark on me."

CASSIUS CLAY on his controversial points victory over Doug Jones.
Both judges favored Clay 5–4–1, but referee gave him an 8-1-1 edge. (John Cottrell, *Man of Destiny*, p.101)

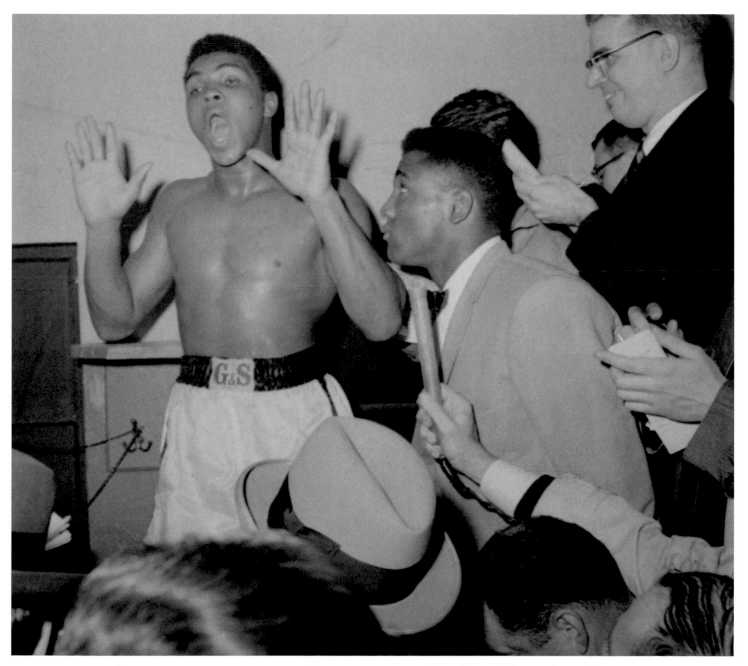

CASSIUS MUGS FOR THE MEDIA AFTER HIS CONTROVERSIAL VICTORY OVER DOUG JONES AT MADISON SQUARE GARDEN.

COOPER
vs. Henry Cooper
June 18, 1963

WEMBLEY STADIUM, LONDON, ENGLAND. KO5.

"If Cooper whups me, I'll get down on my hands and knees, crawl across the ring and kiss his feet.

And then I'll put on a false mustache and beard and take the next jet out of town."

CASSIUS CLAY before his first fight with Henry Cooper. (Jose Torres, *Sting Like a Bee*, p.133)

HOODED AGAINST THE COLD, CASSIUS DOES HIS ROADWORK IN LONDON PRIOR TO HIS FIRST MEETING WITH HENRY COOPER.

"In the first of our two fights, I hit Clay with a genuine left hook with all my power behind it. **He fell on the ropes and slid gently to the canvas.** There was a count of five, and the bell went. There was panic in his corner. **Suddenly, they found Clay had a split glove.** They called the referee over and tried to find a spare pair of gloves.

Easily, that took a half minute, *and to a fit guy, that's a lifetime.*

HENRY COOPER, (*Sports Illustrated*, 9.29.1980)

CLAY WEARS A STUNNED EXPRESSION AFTER BEING FLOORED BY COOPER IN THE FOURTH ROUND.

"They accused me of cutting the gloves. Can you imagine me doing something like that? **There was a rip in the gloves.** *All I did was make it bigger.* They're hunting around for gloves and I'm buying my man time. The way he recuperates, all he needs is a couple of minutes."

ANGLEO DUNDEE on the gloves controversy. (Harry Mullen, *The Book of Boxing Quotations*, p.173)

A BATTERED COOPER WINS THE SYMPATHY OF CLAY.

THREE

Ali the Champion

No one—*not Strauss, Ravel or Stravinsky*

had orchestrated a work

more ingeniously *than the way*

Cassius Clay

stalked and baited

Sonny Liston

into granting him a shot at his heavyweight crown

in the winter of 1964. Even "the Big, Ugly Bear",

as Clay had christened him, failed to realize until too

late how the trap had been set.

CLAY HAMS IT UP WITH THE BEATLES WHO VISITED HIS MIAMI BEACH
TRAINING CAMP BEFORE CHALLENGING SONNY LISTON.

A master of ballyhoo, Clay had dogged Liston's every step, dating back to September, 1962, in Chicago when Liston won the title by disposing of Floyd Patterson in two minutes. Cassius climbed into the ring to immediately challenge the new champion. He would continue his barrage of taunts at the rematch in Las Vegas when Patterson lasted only five more seconds against the menacing ex-con and gang enforcer.

Clay was unimpressed, at least publicly. "Liston is a tramp, I'm the champ," he bellowed. "I want that big ugly bear. I want this big bum as soon as I can get him. I'm tired of talking. If I can't whip him, I'll leave the country." [1]

Clay even took his campaign to Liston's home in an upscale, white enclave in Denver. Disguising his voice, he notified all the Denver papers and television outlets that Cassius Clay was planning to invade Liston's lair in the wee hours of the morning. He then drove his personalized bus, horn blaring, to Sonny's front door, rousing all the neighbors who immediately called the police.

Liston, dressed in polka-dot pajamas and armed with a fireplace poker, charged out his door screaming, "Hey, get out of my yard, you black bastard." [2]

By now, a policeman had Clay collared and said, "If you don't get out of this town in an hour, you're going to jail." [3]

Clay, of course, had the final word, shouting at Liston, "You're no champ. You're a chump. The police and their dogs saved you." [4]

Later, Clay would admit that he recognized Liston as a formidable foe. "Everyone predicted that Liston would destroy me. And he was scary. But it's lack of faith that makes people afraid of meeting challenges, and I believe in myself. I studied his style, went to his training camp and tried to understand what went on inside his head so later on I could mess with his mind.

"And all the time I was talking, talking. That way, I figured I could get Liston so mad that when the fight came he'd try to kill me and forget everything he knew about boxing." [5]

THE PRESENCE OF MUSLIM LEADER MALCOLM X ALMOST CAUSED
THE CANCELATION OF CLAY'S TITLE FIGHT WITH LISTON.

Liston insisted he was not distracted. "My only concern is how I'm going to get my fist outta his big mouth once I get him in the ring." [6]

The heralded match would be hyped as "The Greatest Grudge Match in History", but boxing insiders refused to take Clay seriously, regarding him as a clever-talking puppet manipulated by Madison Avenue hucksters. Conversely, Liston was perceived as every man's worst nightmare—a sullen destroyer with not an ounce of compassion in his bones.

A pre-fight poll showed 43 of 46 boxing writers casting their lot with Liston, a 7–1 favorite. Milton Gross, columnist for the *New York Post*, seemed to speak for the majority when he wrote, "Cassius, the fighter, is a figment of somebody else's imagination. Only in this time of soap bubble promotion could he be taken seriously. The simple fact is that Clay does not know his business. He hasn't had time to learn it. He knows publicity and he is a charmer when it comes to popping off, but he doesn't know what trouble he'll see when Sonny starts working him over with malice afterthought." [7]

While the debate raged, the fight itself began to unravel. Miami promoter, Bill MacDonald, who had paid a $650,000 site fee, threatened to cancel it after learning Clay had been seen in the company of Black Muslims and had personally invited one of its leaders, Malcolm X, to attend the match.

Clay, who, as yet, had not revealed his new identity as Muhammad Ali, had first been spotted the previous fall at a Black Muslim rally in Philadelphia where, according to the *Philadelphia Daily News*, "Elijah Muhammad unleashed a three-hour tirade against the white race and popularly accepted Negro leaders. The Muslim leader called upon Negroes in this country and the entire world to form a solid front against the white race." [8]

A few weeks before his scheduled fight with Liston, Clay left camp accompanied by Malcolm X to attend and speak at a Black Muslim rally in New York. This time his appearance was given front-page coverage in the *New York Herald Tribune*.

When the story created a stir in his home town, Clay told the *Louisville Courier-Journal*, "Sure I talked to the Muslims, and I'm going back again. I'm not going to get killed trying to force myself on people who don't want me. Integration is wrong. The white people don't want it, and the Muslims don't believe in it. So what's wrong about the Muslims?" [9]

Fearing a backlash, MacDonald had pleaded with Clay to publicly announce he was "a true, patriotic, loyal American". [10]

Clay refused, becoming more enamored with the teachings of Malcolm X, who, in turn, voiced his admiration for the fighter's independent spirit. As Malcolm X told George Plimpton, "Not many people know the quality of his mind. He fools them. One forgets that though a clown never imitates a wise man, the wise man can imitate the clown. He is sensitive, very humble, yet shrewd—with as much untapped mental energy as he has physical power. He should be a diplomat." [11]

It would take considerable diplomacy to keep the fight with Liston alive. Malcolm X assured a compromise by agreeing to leave Miami until the day of the fight. It was then that Clay would use one of Malcolm X's favorite African canes as a prop to turn the pre-fight weigh-in into total bedlam, pounding the floor while shouting insults at Liston. Meanwhile, court jester, Drew Bundini, chanted the mantra "Float Like A Butterfly, Sting Like A Bee".

It had all been choreographed by Ali down to the last hysterical scream, fully convincing Liston he was about to face a madman. The act also completely fooled Dr. Alexander Robbins, the Miami Boxing Commission physician, who, after finding Clay's pulse beat soar to 110, declared Clay was "emotionally unbalanced, scared to death, and liable to crack up before he enters the ring". [12]

Ferdie Pacheco, Clay's personal physician and cornerman, knew better. As he confided in author Budd Schulberg: "Cassius is in complete control of himself. He knows exactly what he's doing. It's going to be a very interesting evening." [13]

Indeed. Clay took immediate control of the fight, making the malevolent Liston look like a befuddled novice until the near-fatal fifth round. Liniment on Liston's shoulder had found its way into Clay's eyes. When the fourth round ended, Clay, suspecting skullduggery, began screaming in his corner, "My eyes are burning. I can't see. Cut off my gloves. Show the world what's going on." [14]

Once more, trainer Angelo Dundee saved the day, forcing Clay to sit on his stool while admonishing him, "Forget the bull. This is for the championship. Go get it, man." [15]

His eyes still blurry, Clay managed to keep Liston at arm's length for most of the fifth round. By the sixth round, Liston's face, the object of countless jabs, was badly swollen. He capitulated in his corner before the seventh round, complaining of a sore shoulder.

The morning after, the new heavyweight champion of the world informed a more worshipful audience that he was abandoning the slave name "Clay" and should henceforth be addressed as "Cassius X".

It would be the first step to becoming officially known as Muhammad Ali, a perilous decision as he would soon discover.

CLAY, BEFORE ANNOUNCING HIS NAME CHANGE, IS AN ATTENTIVE LISTENER AT
A SPEECH BY NATION OF ISLAM LEADER, ELIJAH MUHAMMAD.

LISTON '64

vs. Sonny Liston
May 25, 1963

FREEDOM HALL, LOUISVILLE, KENTUCKY. WON 6. (WON WORLD HEAVYWEIGHT TITLE)

"I don't think it's bragging to say I'm something a little special. Where do you think I'd be next week if I didn't know how to shout and holler and make people sit up and take notice? I'd be poor for one thing, and I'd be down in Louisville washing windows or running an elevator and saying 'yes suh', and 'no sur', and knowing my place."

MUHAMMAD ALI, (*Sports Illustrated*, 2.24.1964)

DURING A PRE-FIGHT PHYSICAL, CASSIUS CLAY PROMISES THE WORLD THAT HE
WILL BEAT THE SEEMINGLY INVINCIBLE LISTON IN EIGHT ROUNDS.

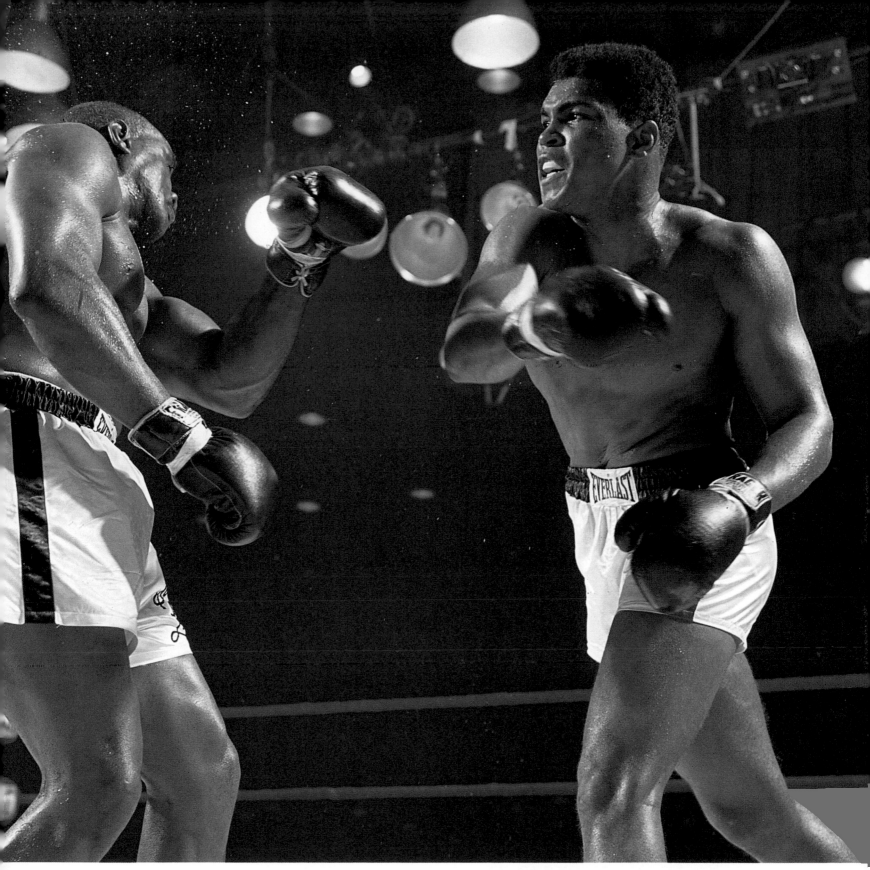

CLAY PROVES TOO QUICK AND ELUSIVE FOR A BEFUDDLED LISTON.

"The simple fact is that Clay does not know his business. He hasn't had time to learn it. He knows publicity and he is a charmer when it comes to popping off. But he doesn't know what trouble he'll see when Sonny starts working him over with malice afterthought." MILTON GROSS, columnist for the *New York Post*.

IT'S CLAY ON THE OFFENSIVE WHILE LISTON
SENSES THE CROWN SLIPPING AWAY.

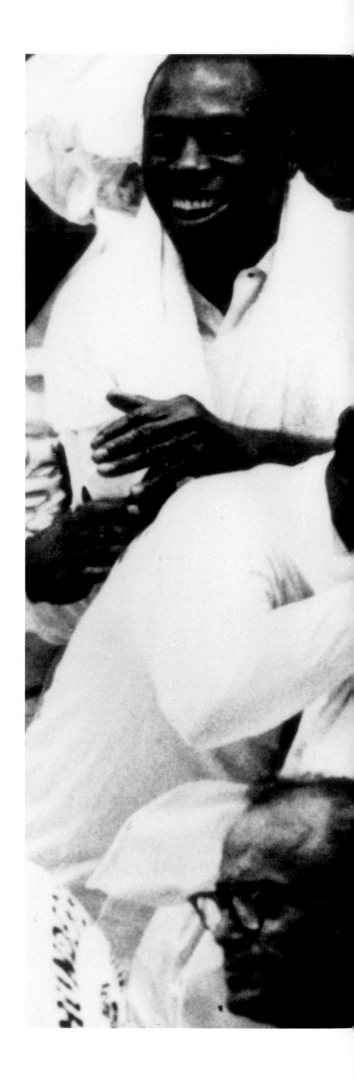

"Did Liston really hurt his shoulder?

I can't say for sure, but I don't think so.

My eyes burned bad in the fifth round.

I could see a little, but not much.

I wanted to stop, but Angelo [Dundee]

pushed me out of the corner."

MUHAMMAD ALI in retrospect.

(Thomas Hauser, *Muhammad Ali, His Life and Times*, p.78)

"You're just a bunch of hypocrites. I told you I was gonna get Liston and I got him. I shook the world and proved all of you wrong.

Now tell me

'Who's the Greatest?'"

MUHAMMAD ALI addressing the media after his victory.
(Richard Durham, *The Greatest*, p.120)

SURROUNDED BY HANDLERS, CLAY WAVES A VICTORIOUS GLOVE AT THE STUNNED AUDIENCE. (OVERLEAF) CLAY PREPARES TO DELIVER AN UPPERCUT AS LISTON TAKES COVER, A TOTALLY UNCHARACTERISTIC POSE FOR A MAN WHO ONCE TERRORIZED THE HEAVYWEIGHT DIVISION

A WIDE-MOUTHED CASSIUS CAN NOW TRUTHFULLY BOAST: "I AM THE GREATEST."

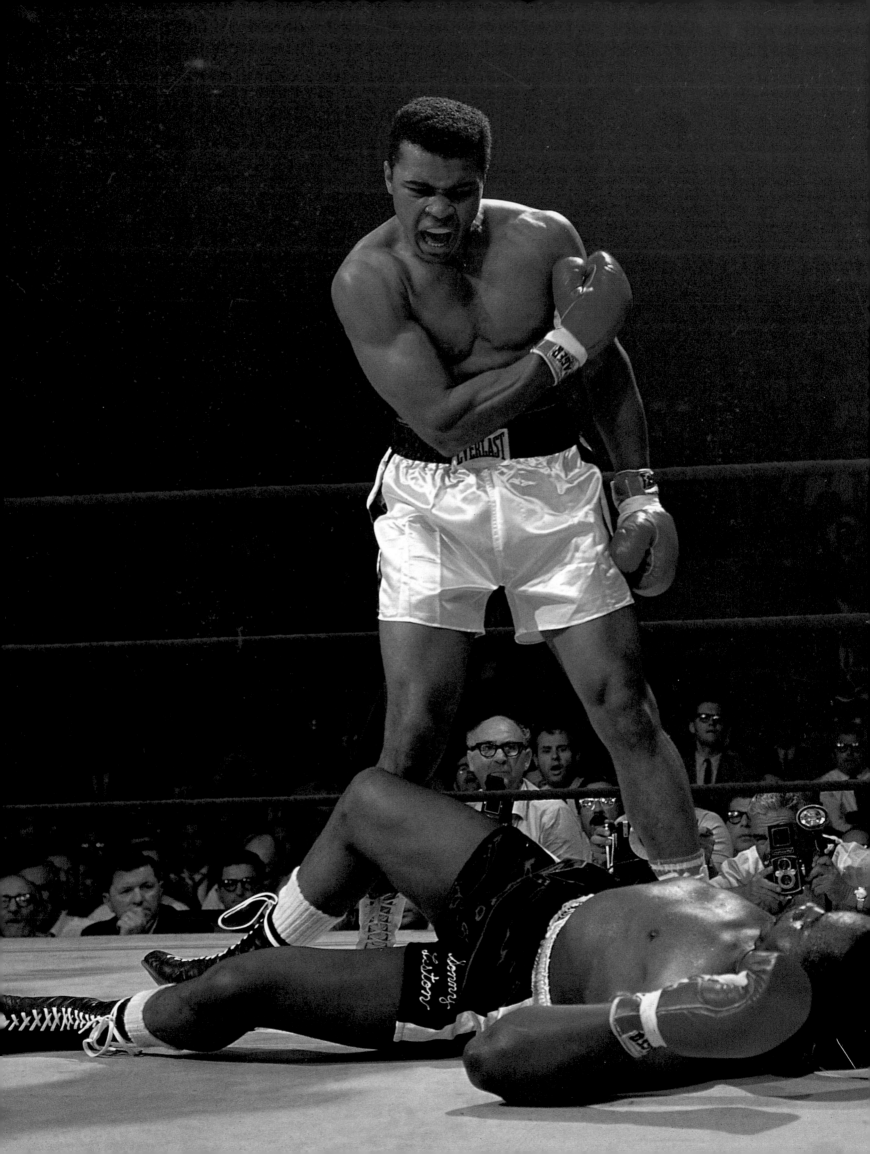

LISTON '65

vs. Sonny Liston
May 25, 1965

ST. DOMINICK'S ARENA, LEWISTON, MAINE. KO1.(RETAINED WORLD HEAVYWEIGHT TITLE)

"The punch jarred him. It was a good punch,

but I didn't think I hit him so hard that he couldn't

have gotten up. Some people said maybe the first

fight was fixed or Liston had a bad shoulder.

So, the second time, I wanted to whip him bad. I didn't want to give

him making any excuses or quitting.

That's why I wanted him to get up."

MUHAMMAD ALI

(Thomas Hauser, *Muhammad Ali, His Life and Times*, p.127)

TO THIS DAY, RINGSIDERS WONDER HOW ALI
MANAGED TO DESTROY LISTON IN THE FIRST
ROUND OF THE CHAMPIONSHIP REMATCH IN
MAINE, MAY 25, 1965. ALI CLAIMS HE USED
THE "ANCHOR PUNCH" AS HIS SECRET
WEAPON—A SHORT, OVERHAND RIGHT.

"He hit him so quick,

the cameras couldn't take it.
He hit him with a shot Liston
couldn't see. They're the ones
that knock you out ..."

Angelo Dundee on the Liston rematch. (unattributed)

Ali takes a victory lap around the ring as referee, Joe Walcott, counts out supine Liston.

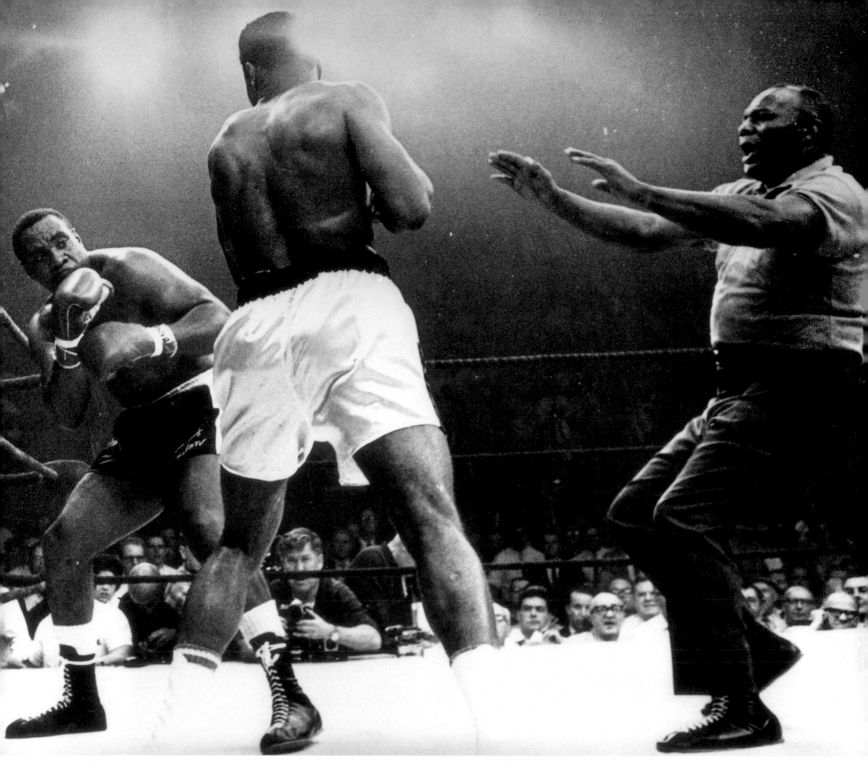

LISTON TRIES TO CONTINUE BATTLE AFTER THE CONFUSION OVER THE "TEN COUNT". WALCOTT REITERATES THAT THE FIGHT IS OVER.

FORMER CHAMPION, FLOYD PATTERSON, CONGRATULATES ALI ON HIS LIGHTNING KO.

vs. Floyd Patterson
November 22, 1965

CONVENTION CENTER, LAS VEGAS, NEVADA, KO12. (RETAINED WORLD HEAVYWEIGHT TITLE)

"I didn't carry him one bit.

He took my best punches and didn't fall. If I knock him out fast, you'd say it was fixed.

If I knock him out slow, I'm a brute. I'm wrong if I do. I'm wrong if I don't."

MUHAMMAD ALI. Ali was accused of carrying Patterson to punish him for continuing
to address him as "Cassius Clay". (*New York Times*, 11.24.1965)

CRITICS CLAIM THAT ALI TORTURED FLOYD PATTERSON FOR FAILING TO ACKNOWLEDGE HIS MUSLIM NAME.
THROUGHOUT THE FIGHT, ALI TAUNTED PATTERSON, WHO WAS PLAGUED BY A SORE BACK.

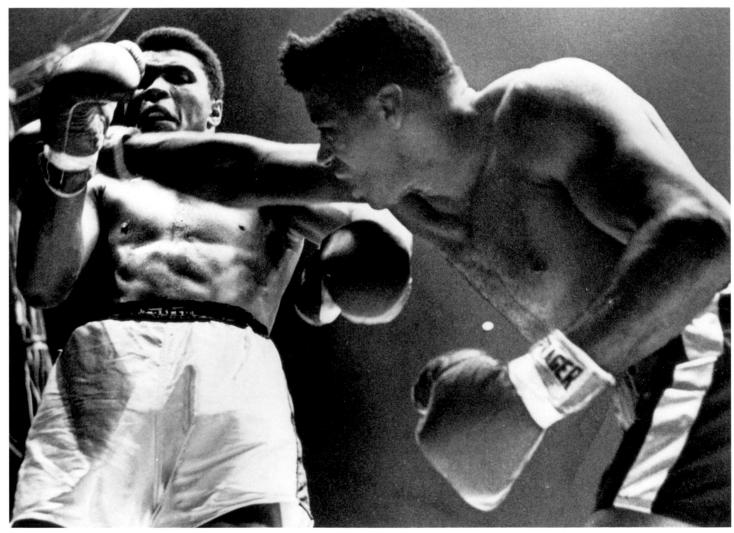

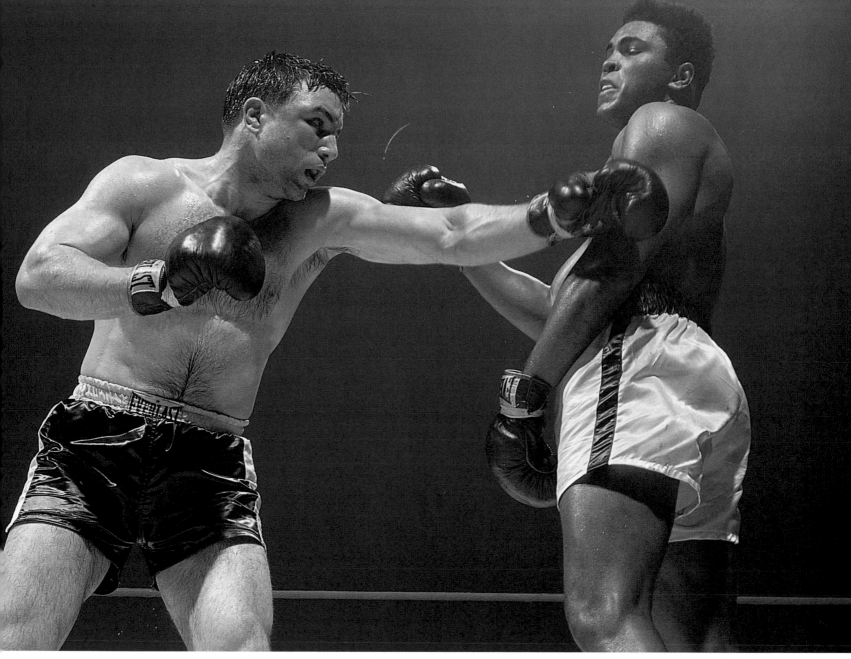

CANADA'S GEORGE CHUVALO PROVED A RUGGED CHALLENGER IN GOING THE 15-ROUND DISTANCE WITH ALI.

CHUVALO '66

vs. George Chuvalo
March 29,1966

MAPLE LEAF GARDENS, TORONTO, CANADA. WON 15. (RETAINED WORLD HEAVYWEIGHT TITLE)

"With all the traveling I did before the fight, I didn't have a chance to work on the heavy bag.

The hardest thing I punched since I fought Patterson was Chuvalo's head."

MUHAMMAD ALI, *(Associated Press,* 3.30.1966)

"Ali didn't know too much for me.

It was a physical thing that let me down

—having prominent bones and weak tissue around the eyes."

HENRY COOPER after his second fight with Ali.

(Harry Mullen, *The Book of Boxing Quotations*, p.122)

ALI GIVES COOPER A PLAYFUL KNOCK ON THE CHIN BEFORE THEIR 1966 REMATCH IN LONDON, ENGLAND.

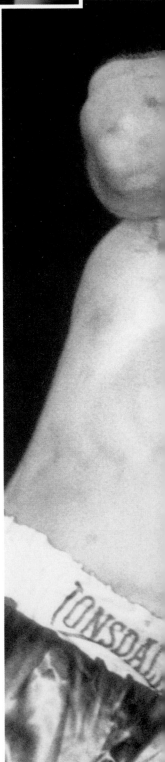

ALI AND COOPER FIGHT AT CLOSE QUARTERS.

COOPER '66

vs. Henry Cooper
May 21, 1966

HIGHBURY STADIUM, LONDON, ENGLAND. KO6. (RETAINED WORLD HEAVYWEIGHT TITLE)

"OUR 'ENERY" GIVES HIS BEST BEFORE A HORRIBLE CUT OVER HIS LEFT EYE IN THE SIXTH ROUND ENDED THE TITLE CHALLENGE.

"I went into the ring expecting to go the full 15 rounds. I reckon I'm as good as the rest.

But Ali is different. *He's more than the greatest.*

I'm disgusted with myself. To get knocked out that way isn't good enough … I've never been booed out of the ring like that before. I was certain I could go the distance. But after the third round, I can't remember much. Everything happened so quickly. I don't know what punch actually got me. There was such a flurry, I can't remember anything else."

BRIAN LONDON, (*Associated Press*, 8.7.1966)

ALI APPEARS TO BE DREAMING OF BIGGER CHALLENGES BEFORE BUTCHERING BRIAN LONDON.

vs. Brian London
August 6,1966

EARL'S COURT STADIUM, LONDON, ENGLAND. KO3. (RETAINED WORLD HEAVYWEIGHT TITLE)

"I'd like a return match, but only if you put a 56-pound weight on each ankle."

BRIAN LONDON, visiting Ali's dressing room after the fight. (Harry Mullan, *The Book of Boxing Quatations*)

MILDENBERGER '66

vs. Karl Mildenberger
September 10, 1966

WALD STADIUM, FRANKFURT, GERMANY. KO12. (RETAINED WORLD HEAVYWEIGHT TITLE)

"I fought my best, but the cut under my left eye made it impossible. I really couldn't see him from the ninth round on.

Except for the time when he floored me just before the bell ended the fifth round, I was happy the way things were going.

When he put me down in the 10th, that was when I knew I was in serious trouble." KARL MILDENBERGER, (*Associated Press*, 9.10.1966)

GERMANY'S KARL MILDENBERGER PROVED AN EASY TARGET FOR ALI, BUT SURVIVED UNTIL THE 12TH ROUND IN THE FRANKFURT BOUT.

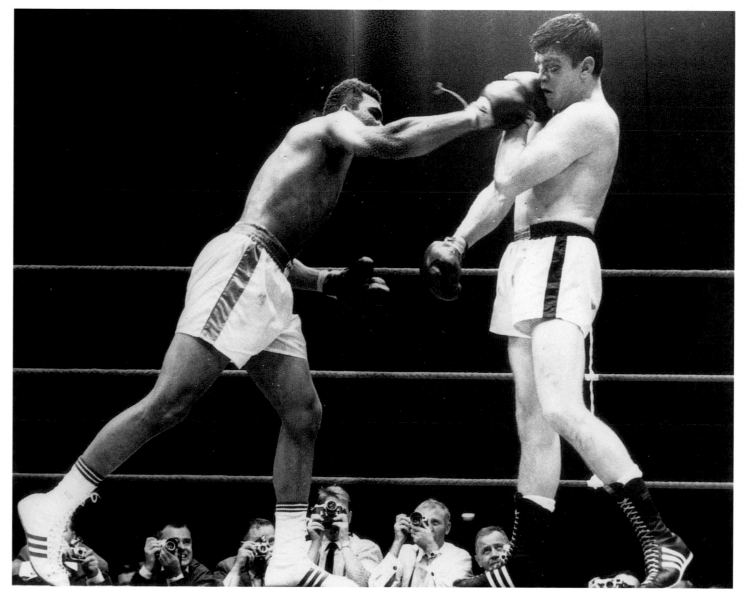

vs. Cleveland Williams
November 14, 1966

ASTRODOME, HOUSTON, TEXAS. KO3. (RETAINED WORLD HEAVYWEIGHT TITLE)

"He's a real good puncher, but he had nothing to punch at.

I thought the referee should have stopped it earlier."

MUHAMMAD ALI, commenting on the fight after Williams had been knocked down four times. (*Associated Press*, 11.14.1966)

CLEVELAND WILLIAMS TAKES IT STRAIGHT ON THE JAW IN A LOPSIDED LOSS TO ALI.
(RIGHT) ALI WAS AT HIS BEST IN FLOORING WILLIAMS FOUR TIMES ON HIS WAY TO A THIRD-ROUND KNOCK-OUT.

"Before the fight, I was confident I could win. Then I got thumbed and everything changed. **I thought the thumbing was intentional** … *Ali had a plan for everybody he fought.* And when the stakes are high, I guess people do certain things. What he did was, he grabbed me around the neck and poked his thumb in my eye around three times. Then he got the top rope and rubbed my head against it … And what happened was, his thumb went up and pushed my eye down to the bone and I had double vision. I couldn't fight my regular fight because I was seeing two guys and didn't know which one to jab. So I fought a kind of 'peek-a-boo' style, walking straight toward him, and you just couldn't beat him that way."

ERNIE TERRELL, (Thomas Hauser, *Muhammad Ali, His Life and Times*, p.164)

THINGS GOT UGLY BETWEEN ALI AND ERNIE TERRELL, WHO ACCUSED MUHAMMAD OF EMPLOYING ILLEGAL TACTICS.

"It just never happened. **People saw me fight for 20 years,** *and I was never a dirty fighter.* I'm not denying I tried to get him to say my proper name. I was bad that night where that was concerned But the thumbing and rubbing never happened."

MUHAMMAD ALI's rebuttal to the thumbing claim. (Thomas Hauser, *Muhammad Ali, His Life and Times*, p.165)

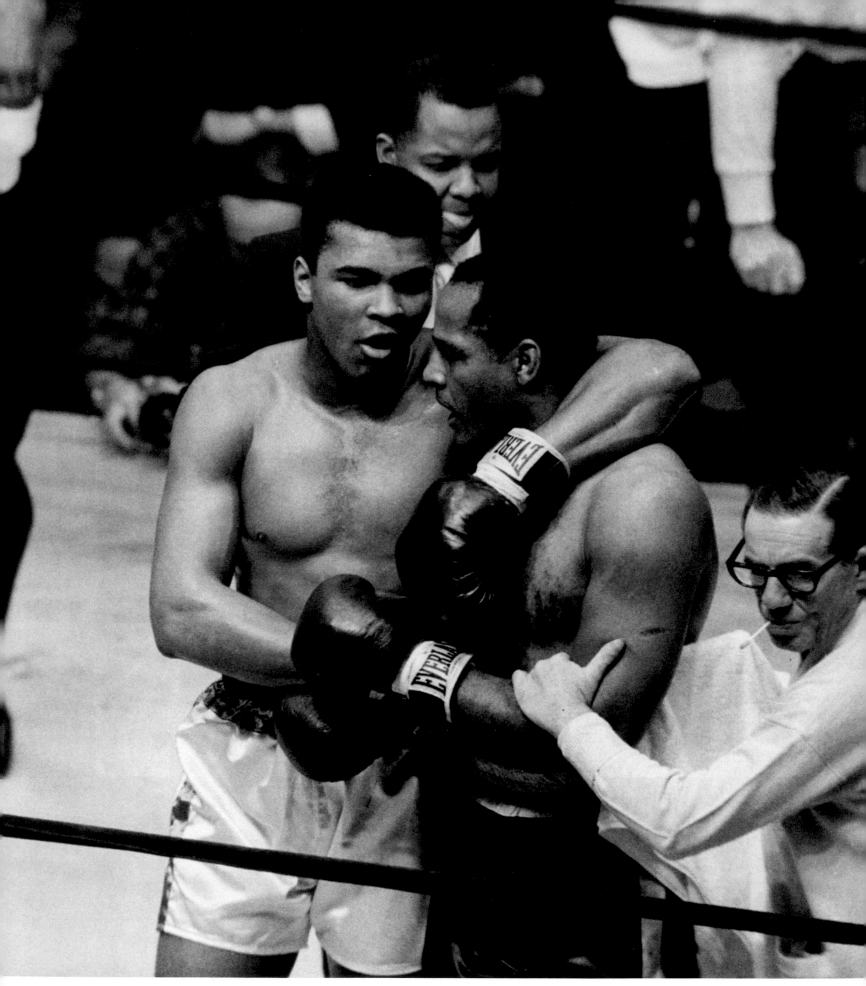

Ali consoles Zora Folley after giving him a boxing lesson at Madison Square Garden.

FOLLEY '67

vs. Zora Folley
May 22, 1967

MADISON SQUARE GARDEN, NEW YORK CITY. KO7. (RETAINED WORLD HEAVYWEIGHT TITLE)

"This guy had a style all his own. It's far ahead of any fighter today.

How could Dempsey, Tunney or any of them keep up with him.

Louis was too slow. Marciano would never get away from Ali's jab.

There's no way to train for what he does. *The move, the speed, the punches and the way he changes style every time you think you have him figured.*

The right hands he hit me with had no business landing, but they did.

They came from nowhere. Many times he was in the wrong position,

and he hit me anyway. The knockdown punch was so fast I never saw it.

He's the trickiest fighter I've ever seen. He could write the

book on boxing, and anyone that fights him should read it."

ZORA FOLLEY, (*Sports Illustrated*, 6.10.1967)

"CASSIUS CLAY—ARMY."

It was a simple command.

In a crowded Houston office serving as a local draft board Army Lt. S. Steven

Dunkley stood before Muhammad Ali (a.k.a. Cassius Clay) and said,

"You will take one step forward
as your name
and service are called
and such a step
will constitute your induction
into the Armed Forces
as indicated."

ALI ARRIVES AT THE INDUCTION CENTER IN HOUSTON WHERE HE WAS TO MAKE HIS STAND.

A roomful of spectators watched anxiously as Ali remained in place, his usually animated face impassive. Again, the lieutenant called his name, only to be met by the same resistance.

In one unspoken, symbolic moment, Ali had managed to change the politics of America and widen the racial gulf in a way that would later be categorized "a national trauma". [1]

No longer would the glib, 22-year-old, heavyweight champion with his childlike doggerel and carefree ways be pictured as a court jester. The laughter had ended. By refusing induction during the Vietnam crisis, Ali was branded as anti-war, anti-government and anti-establishment—an enemy of the state. A nation divided by race viewed him as either a traitor or a martyr.

But the U.S. government did not wait for a consensus. For rejecting his call to arms, Ali was sentenced to five years in prison and a fine of $10,000. History and the Supreme Court, after a number of appeals, would vindicate him, but only after more than three years in virtual exile.

For this was a turbulent time in America. Robert Kennedy, the President's brother, and Black leaders Martin Luther King and Malcolm X, who had once served as Ali's mentor, were all assassinated. It was not a time for rebellion, and few movers and shakers in the country were sympathetic with Ali's ties to the Black Muslims, who were widely viewed as "a race-hate cult".

They preferred their black heroes to be humble and patriotic in the mold of Joe Louis, who, while serving as little more than an entertainer for the troops in World War II, rallied his fellow Americans with the assurance, "God is on our side."

So, without due process, Ali was stripped of his heavyweight crown, banned from fighting in the United States, placed under surveillance by the FBI and relieved of his passport and a chance to practice his livelihood abroad. A unique fighter who could "float like a butterfly and sting like a bee", he was now indefinitely grounded.

In 1964, when he was still known by his slave name of Clay, he received a 1-Y deferment from his Louisville draft board after twice failing the Army aptitude test. A somewhat embarrassed Clay was heard to utter, "I said I was 'The Greatest', not the smartest." [2]

When the United States became firmly enmeshed in the Vietnam War, standards were reduced and Clay was re-classified 1-A, making him eligible for service. Ali then sought an exemption as a conscientious objector, but was rejected on the grounds his adopted religion was "racist and political".

Ali replied, "I believe in Allah and in peace. I know where I'm going and I know the truth, and I don't have to be what you want me to be ... I'm free to be what I want. You can't condemn a man for wanting peace. If you do, you condemn peace itself. A rooster crows only when he sees the light. I have seen the light, and I'm crowing." [3]

A bit too much for the public's taste, especially when he made his infamous "I Ain't Got No Quarrel With Them Viet Cong" comment after being re-classified 1-A. The response was immediate, resulting in the cancellation of his title-unifying match in Chicago with Ernie Terrell, then recognized as the World Boxing Association champion.

Jingoistic politicians and national columnists moved quickly to condemn Ali's stand. Milton Gross of the *New York Post* seemed to speak for the majority when he wrote, "As a fighter Cassius is good. As a man, he can't compare to some of the kids slogging through the rice paddies where the names are stranger than Muhammad Ali." [4]

Even a pair of former heavyweight champions joined in the furor. Gene Tunney, who served as a Marine overseas in World War I, admonished Ali, "You have disgraced your title and the American flag and the principles for which it stands. Apologize for your remarks or you'll be barred from the ring." [5]

And Dempsey, who was also branded a draft dodger during his championship reign, warned Ali that it was no longer safe to walk the streets of America.

But Ali was never one to hide. In fact, he was quick to answer his critics, wondering why Dempsey and Tunney never defended their titles against a black challenger, and, more importantly, why they remained silent in the Twenties when the Ku Klux Klan made a popular sport of lynching in the South.

The searing heat of criticism only seemed to strengthen his conviction. "I've left the sports pages for the front page," he said. "I'm being tested by Allah. If I pass this test, I'll come out stronger than ever. I've got no jails, no power, no government, but 600 million Muslims are giving me strength. Why can't I worship as I want in America. All I want is justice. Will I get that from history?" [6]

He found a new platform to preach his beliefs by touring colleges across the country where draft-eligible students were more sympathetic to his anti-war views. In between court appeals and attending Muslim meetings, Ali supplemented his income by appearing in the Broadway musical *Buck White*, helping to write his autobiography, making a documentary of his life called "a.k.a." and staging a computer battle with former champion, Rocky Marciano. The United States version had a bloodied "Rock" knocking out Ali in the 13th round while, in Europe, where Ali was still a cult figure, Muhammad proved victorious.

And the more the government tightened its noose, the more, it seemed, Ali strengthened his ties to the Black Muslims. By now, he had rid himself of the Louisville millionaires who had launched his pro career and cast his lot with Herbert Muhammad, the son of the prophet, Elijah Muhammad. It was a move that was met with disapproval by both Ali's parents. It would evolve into bitter arguments with his father, who openly accused the Black Muslims of stealing his son's money.

Ironically, in 1969, Ali was also suspended by the Black Muslims for publicly expressing a desire to return to the ring if the right offer presented itself.

Elijah Muhammad made his position clear in the Nation of Islam's paper, *The Messenger.* "Mr. Muhammad Ali acted the fool," he wrote. "He wants a place in the sports world. He shall not be recognized by us under the holy name Muhammad Ali. He will be known as Cassius Clay. This statement is to tell the world that we, the Muslims, are not with Muhammad Ali, in his desire to work in sports for the sake of a 'leetle' money. Allah has power over the heavens and the earth. He is sufficient for us." [7]

A contrite Ali, with help from Herbert Muhammad, soon returned to the flock. He would eventually win his battle in the Supreme Court and be free to fight again under his chosen name. During a month's visit to Africa in 1964, he had discovered the power he possessed outside the ring. In Ghana, his every public appearance was greeted by huge crowds of adoring followers chanting, "Ali, Ali, Ali."

It had helped him maintain his faith through three-and-a-half years of political exile. He was reborn. The second coming of Muhammad Ali was about to begin.

ALI SUPPORTERS MARCH IN HIS SUPPORT AFTER HE REFUSED INDUCTION INTO THE ARMY ON RELIGIOUS GROUNDS.

"I ain't got no quarrel with them Viet Cong."

MUHAMMAD ALI, explaining resistance to being drafted. (*New York Times*, 2.18.1966)

ALI INFORMS THE MEDIA THAT HE IS STICKING TO HIS ANTI-WAR CONVICTIONS
DESPITE THE THREAT OF JAIL AND THE LOSS OF HIS HEAVYWEIGHT CROWN.

A NATION BECOMES DIVIDED WHEN MUHAMMAD ALI SAYS THAT HE HAS "NO QUARREL WITH THEM VIET CONG".

"The power structure seems to want to starve me out. I mean, the punishment, five years in jail, $10,000 fine ain't enough. **They want to stop me from working, not only in this country, but out of it.**"

MUHAMMAD ALI, after being re-classified 1-A by the selective Service Board. (*New York Times*, 2.18.1966)

"He is a fighter who stands for something,

and that's the mark of a fighter.

He doesn't stand neutral.

He's a rights fighter also, *like me.*

The man who stands neutral stands for nothing."

ARCHIE MOORE defending Ali's anti-war stand.

SPORTSCASTER HOWARD COSELL (LEFT) WAS ONE OF THE FEW
MEMBERS OF THE MEDIA WHO SUPPORTED ALI'S RIGHT TO DEFY
INDUCTION INTO MILITARY SERVICE.

FIVE

Back in the Ring

"I'm not just fighting one man. I'm fighting a lot of men, showing a lot of them

here is one man they couldn't defeat, couldn't conquer, *one they didn't see* **big and fat and flat on his back.**

If Quarry beats me, he'll be a great man. It won't be just a loss for me.

So many people will be rejoicing in the streets and at home.

But millions will also be sad, like they've been defeated themselves.

If I lose, I'll be called a bum, how I joined the wrong movement

and they misled me. *So, in a way, I'm fighting for my freedom."*

MUHAMMAD ALI, speaking before his first fight in over three years.

The Return

The huge poster outside the ramshackle Municipal Auditorium in Atlanta looked more like an advertisement for a play than the prize fight that took place inside the arena the memorable night of October 26, 1970.

Muhammad Ali, who had enjoyed a brief taste of the world of make-believe performing on Broadway in the musical *Buck White*, dominated the poster designed by artist Leroy Neiman. He looked bigger than life, standing straight as a toy soldier with his head proudly held high and his gloves dangling defiantly by his sides, as if daring someone to knock him off the mountaintop. Conversely, Jerry Quarry, the hand-chosen opponent for Ali's first fight in more than three years, was portrayed as a brash Irishman, his hair awry and a heavy stubble hiding his otherwise handsome face.

It was as it should be. This was Ali's show with Quarry acting strictly as a sideman. Ali was playing the role of the martyr, fighting the first of his Holy Wars. It was Ali versus the Establishment that robbed him of his title and best years as a champion, plus untold millions of dollars because of his religious beliefs and stand against an immoral war.

During his exile, friends beseeched him to give up the good fight. Rocky Marciano told Ali's wife, Belinda, "Tell Muhammad to stop torturing himself. Get him out of boxing and forget the whole thing." And Belinda replied, "He won it in the ring and he'll lose it in the ring. That's the only way he'll give up his crown." [1]

He was clearly a man on a mission. "I'm not fighting just one man," he said. "I'm fighting a lot of men, showing a lot of them here is one man they couldn't defeat, couldn't conquer, one they didn't see big and fat and flat on his back.

"If Quarry beats me, he'll be a great man. It won't just be a loss for me. So many people will be rejoicing in the streets and at home. But millions will also be sad, like they've been defeated themselves. All of this just over a fight. If I lose, I'll be called a bum and tossed in jail the rest of my life. So, in a way, I'm fighting for my freedom." [2]

Ironically, he would begin his heralded comeback in Atlanta, the cradle of the South and the symbol of the lifelong injustices that had compelled Ali to join the Black Muslim separatist sect. But, by now, the political climate in America had changed dramatically. Anti-establishment groups, like the Black Panthers, were no longer considered a major threat, and more and more people were supporting Ali's disapproval of the Vietnam War. He had become a political and social force for a wide audience that had little interest in boxing and would find his way back in the ring before Secretary of State, Henry Kissinger, predicted peace was at hand.

But Ali did not thump his chest in self-righteousness. Reflecting on his exile, he said, "I never thought of myself as great when I refused to go into the Army. There were people who thought the war in Vietnam was right. And those people, who went to war, acted just as brave as I did. There were people who tried to put me in jail. Some of them were hypocrites, but others did what they thought was proper and I can't condemn them for following their conscience either.

"Standing up for my religion made me happy; it wasn't a sacrifice. I knew people in Vietnam were dying. When people went to Vietnam and came home with one leg and couldn't get a job, that was a sacrifice. Some people thought I was a hero, some thought what I did was wrong. But everything I did was according to my conscience. I wasn't trying to be a leader. I just wanted to be free. I wanted America to be America." [3]

Victories in court over voting rights had empowered blacks in the South, opening the door for Ali's comeback. He gained the support of Leroy Johnson, a black legislator in

Georgia who controlled a large block of voters in Atlanta. Johnson used this clout to persuade Atlanta's popular Jewish mayor, Sam Massell, to back Ali's fight with Quarry.

Ali had already tested the water in Atlanta by staging an exhibition at Morehouse College, a traditional black school, without significant backlash by the white populace. But this would prove an entirely different matter.

Training for the fight in the outskirts of Atlanta, Ali and his entourage received numerous threats and, finally, survived a scary night of rifle fire before state troopers intervened.

The biggest threat to canceling the match came from Georgia Governor, Lester Maddox, a staunch segregationist, who declared "A Day of Mourning" and urged all the citizens of his state to boycott the fight. He had also sought to kill the fight by invoking a state ordinance dating back to post-Civil War days that prohibited bouts between blacks and whites. The Atlanta City Council worked quickly in secrecy to change the rule and keep the fight alive.

The pre-fight scene in the heart of Atlanta was a spine-tingling "happening". Black leaders from across the country rallied in support of Ali. The political front brought civil rights leaders Whitney Young, Coretta Scott King, Ralph Abernathy, Julian Bond and Jesse Jackson, while Sidney Poitier and Bill Cosby represented the world of entertainment, celebrating a gifted performer's return to center stage.

But there were also the common folk—men decked out in full-length fur coats and their women in gossamer evening gowns. As boxing historian, Bert Sugar, recalled, "People were arriving in hand-painted limousines, dressed in colors and styles I'd never seen. They'd come for the return of Muhammad Ali, and there was no doubt in their minds that he'd win. They weren't boxing fans; they were idolators." [4]

Still, no one was quite sure how Ali would perform after such a long absence from the ring. Ali himself, sought the opinion of Dr. Ferdie Pacheco, who served as his personal ring physician. Said Pacheco, "Time takes a toll more than an irrevocable beating. The body wears, changes even more when it's not active. Reflexes slow down and they go. No one can tell how long a fighter's got, not when you deal with a super-athlete. We can examine the body but not the psyche, and that's where the real secret is locked." [5]

There was no question of Ali's mental state when he entered the ring to face Quarry. He was a man on a mission, bearing the ghost of Jack Johnson, the first black heavyweight champion at the turn of the century. Johnson served as a role model for Ali because of his fierce independence and a long and bitter battle with the government that eventually forced him to seek asylum abroad.

The fight itself was almost an anti-climax. The opening round was vintage Ali. He rewarded the partisan crowd with a familiar display of dazzling hand and foot speed, frustrating his stalking foe. Quarry provided a scary moment in the second round with a brutal hook to the body that seemed to slow Ali's momentum. But a slashing right cross in the third round opened a gaping wound over Quarry's left eye, leaving referee Tony Perez with no choice but to stop the fight.

Ali had seized the day. But his eye was now on a far bigger prize, the championship belt Joe Frazier had claimed in absentia. First, there would be a tense struggle with Argentine strongman Oscar Bonavena, but "The Fight of the Century" between two unbeaten, charismatic heavyweights was the battle the whole world anticipated.

"*I was nervous before it started,* tense like I like to be. There was excitement in the live crowd and I'm sure it was that way all over the country, all over the world—even in Russia."

MUHAMMAD ALI, (*Baltimore Sun,* 10.26.1970)

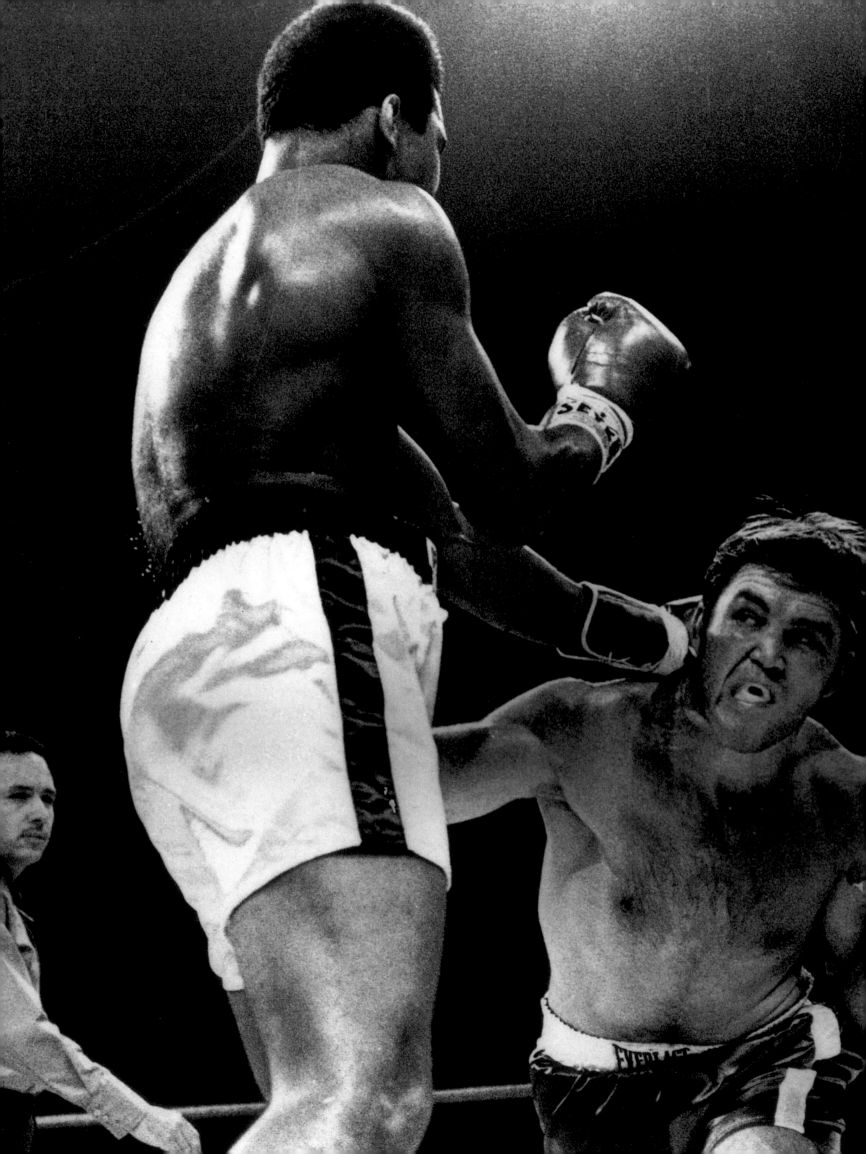

QUARRY '70

vs. Jerry Quarry
October 26, 1970

MUNICIPAL AUDITORIUM, ATLANTA, GEORGIA. KO3.

"I wasn't fighting for any race, creed or color that night. I was fighting for money. My heritage was *The Grapes of Wrath*. **Before getting into boxing, I was making $99 a week changing tires on Greyhound buses. To fight Ali, I got the biggest purse of my life—$300,000.** If I'd won, and I thought I would, I'd have made millions. None of the noise surrounding the fight bothered me. The crowd was 90 percent black and for Ali, but that didn't motivate or intimidate me. I wasn't fighting against a symbol. I was fighting a fighter who had two arms and two legs just like me."

JERRY QUARRY before his fight with Ali. (Thomas Hauser, *Muhammad Ali, His Life and Times*, p.211)

DESPITE A THREE-YEAR ABSENCE FROM THE RING, ALI STILL PROVED TOO QUICK FOR AN AGRESSIVE JERRY QUARRY TO SUCCESSFULLY LAUNCH HIS COMEBACK WITH A THIRD-ROUND KO.

CIVIL RIGHTS LEADERS RALPH ABERNATHY AND CORETTA SCOTT KING HELP ALI CELEBRATE HIS SUCCESSFUL COMEBACK AGAINST QUARRY.

"I needed the work, and the longer it lasted, the easier it was to land punches. If Quarry hadn't been cut so bad, he probably could have gone ten rounds or so. I wish he had …

Quarry was a good boxer. He tries to sucker you in for a big punch, but he never landed one on me."

MUHAMMAD ALI at the post-fight press conference. (*Baltimore Sun*, 10.26.1970)

BONAVENA '70

vs. Oscar Bonavena
December 12,1970

MADISON SQUARE GARDEN, NEW YORK CITY. KO15.

IT WAS LIFE AND DEATH FOR ALI BEFORE HE SUMMONED
A RESERVOIR OF STRENGTH TO FINISH ARGENTINE
STRONGMAN OSCAR BONAVENA IN THE 15TH ROUND.

Publicists for Madison Square Garden,

in a master stroke of understatement, simply called it

"The Fight".

Co-promoter, Jerry Perenchio, a newcomer toprofessional boxing, labeled it

"one of the greatest entertainment events in history".

The former press agent for Elizabeth Taylor gushed,

"It's like Gone With The Wind. You could hold it

in a supermarket and people would still come." [1]

Muhammad Ali, never to be undone, proclaimed it

"the greatest event in the history of planet Earth". [2]

The *literati* compared the impending battle to **Cain versus Abel.**

Ali-Frazier I, the night of March 8, 1971 at New York's Madison Square Garden was all that and more. In the aftermath of the historic match, Harry Markson, the Garden's long-time director of boxing, said, "It was probably the most glittering night ever held in the arena. Unlike most Super Bowls, this held up to everything expected and well beyond it." [3]

The "Fight of the Century" attracted a glittering mob of celebrities and VIPs. Frank Sinatra was working as an accredited photographer for *Life*, joined at ringside by Joe DiMaggio, Apollo astronaut Alan Shepard, David Frost and most of the Kennedy clan. The media had 760 representatives, with an additional 500 requests rejected.

The crowd of 20,455 set a Garden record, not to mention the millions around the world who watched the fight on closed-circuit television. But it was the record purses of $5 million, divided evenly by the two fighters, that raised the most eyebrows.

As *New York Post* columnist Milton Gross wrote, "This must be the age of absurdity or incredibility, if not insanity. The money is something out of a Hollywood extravaganza. Never before in the history of entertainment have any performers been offered $5 million for a one-shot thing." [4]

The universal interest in this rare match between two unbeaten heavyweights—Frazier, the reigning champion, and Ali, the former heavyweight king who had spent over three years in exile for refusing service in the Vietnam War—far exceeded the usual bloodlust of hardcore boxing fans.

For, in a broad sense, this was a morality play being played off-Broadway. Ali, who had adopted the Muslim faith shortly before winning the title from Sonny Liston in 1964, was cast in the role not only of the anti-establishment hero, but also of the showman with a huge ego, whose unusual speed and artistry had made him the Nureyev of the prize ring.

Frazier, one of 17 children of a South Carolina sharecropper, strengthened his muscular body working in a Philadelphia slaughterhouse before, like Ali, winning an Olympic gold medal. He was popularly portrayed as a no-nonsense, blue-collar worker who let his sledge-hammer fists do all the talking.

Frazier hated Ali, and for good reason. In the pre-fight buildup, Ali had called him "ignorant", a "gorilla" and "Uncle Tom", a black man representing the latest "White Hope". The mean-spirited attack brought an angry response from the media.

Dick Young of the *New York Daily News*, wrote, "He has run out of white opponents, and now he feels the need to whitewash Frazier. And so, for the next weeks, Muhammad Ali, in his charming and shrewd way, will paint Joe Frazier as the standard bearer of the white bigots, as the white man's lackey, the betrayer of his people. It's a cruel and unworthy thing he does." [5]

Frazier, who would never forgive Ali for demeaning him, turned the fight into a personal crusade. He was more than willing for Ali to play to the crowds and expend his energy in pre-fight hyperbole. In fact, Ali was so besieged by admirers when he roamed the streets of New York, the Garden boxing executives felt, for his self-preservation, that he should spend the day of the fight in one of the arena dressing rooms.

"It was like he was the 'Prisoner of Seventh Avenue', his trainer, Angelo Dundee, said, alluding to the Broadway show. "He slept on a cot and had to call out for food to be delivered. He never left the joint the whole day. Instead of walking the street he was counting stairs, and I think it wore him down mentally." [6]

But Ali had not shown the slightest case of nerves in the days leading up to the fight. He was his usual playful self and turned the pre-fight physical examination into a hilarious scene resembling an old vaudeville act, with the New York Boxing Commission doctor playing the straight man.

Doctor:	"When was your last fight?"
Ali:	*"You mean you really don't remember?"*
Doctor:	*"*Is there any reason you know of why you shouldn't fight Monday?"
Ali:	*"The only reason I can think of is if Joe Frazier doesn't show up."*
Doctor:	"Bend down and touch your toes 20 times!"
Ali:	*"Let me see you do it first, Doc."*
Doctor:	"Open your mouth and say, 'Ah'"
Ali:	*"Why do all the cameramen want this picture so bad?"* [7]

And so it went right up until the opening bell when Frazier gained sweet revenge for all his days of humiliation. After the first few rounds, in which Ali was able to jab and move out of harm's way, it became painstakingly clear that all the years he had spent in limbo had robbed him of his speed and elusiveness against a relentless aggressor.

By the middle rounds, he was forced to stand toe-to-toe with Frazier, and, when fatigue enveloped him, he tried to buy time resting against the ropes while Frazier bludgeoned his body. "My guy started playing around," Dundee remembered. "Patting Frazier on the head, hamming it up and checking the people at ringside. I told him to stop messing around. While he was playing, Frazier came on strong." [8]

Ali's legs turned rubbery in the 11th round after catching a monstrous left hook flush on the chin, but, miraculously, with a burst of energy, he rallied to win several of the late rounds.

Ali danced out of his corner to start the 15th and final round, only to again move into the path of a wicked left hook that sent him crashing to the floor, with only the ropes saving him from joining the ringside photographers. "That's the punch that did it, the one that blew out the candles," Ali's cornerman and cheerleader, Bundini Brown, would sadly recall. [9]

Ali would beat the count, using all his guile to survive the final minutes. But he knew in his heart that he had suffered his first professional loss. A number of well-wishers, including Diana Ross, tried to say otherwise. But Ali, speaking through a swollen jaw, said, "I never thought of losing, and never thought I could. But when it happens, you have to give the man his due. There are more important things to mourn than Ali losing a fight. I'll probably be a better man for it. I'm not crying and my friends shouldn't cry." [10]

Ironically, in defeat, Ali had gained wider respect than in any of his ring triumphs. Norman Mailer, covering the fight for *Life* magazine, wrote, "Ali had shown America what he hoped for was secretly true. He was a man. He could beat moral and physical torture and he could stand." [11]

A jubilant Frazier had gained his pound of flesh in a memorable brawl for the ages. And next week's cover of *Sports Illustrated* shrieked "The End of the Ali Legend". But this was only the first of a classic ring trilogy with Frazier, and the indomitable Ali would inevitably have the final word.

(LEFT) DESPITE AN UNUSUALLY LARGE ENTOURAGE, INCLUDING BUNDINI BROWN (RIGHT), ALI PREFERRED TAPING HIS OWN HANDS BEFORE DONNING HIS GLOVES.

FRAZIER '71
vs. Joe Frazier
March 8, 1971

MADISON SQUARE GARDEN, NEW YORK CITY. L15. (FOR THE WORLD HEAVYWEIGHT TITLE)

"People want to see me whipped because I'm arrogant, because of the draft, because of my religion and for other reasons I even don't know about … But **I thrive on pressure. If there's no controversy, I can't get ready.** He'll be shaking, and I'll win easy." MUHAMMAD ALI, (*Baltimore Sun*, 3.7.1971)

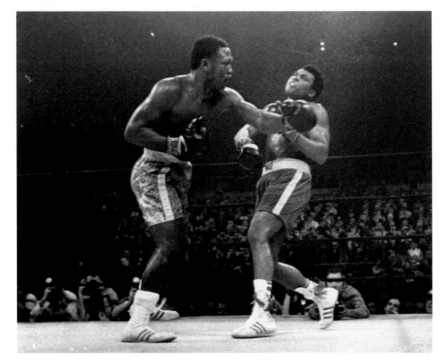

JOE FRAZIER ADMINSTERS ONE OF HIS CLASSIC LEFT HOOKS TO CATCH A RETREATING ALI. (RIGHT) ALI WASN'T PRACTICING "ROPE-A-DOPE" IN THIS INSTANCE WHILE TESTING FRAZIER'S FIREPOWER.

"Frazier's no real champion. Nobody wants to talk to him. Oh, maybe President Nixon will call him if he wins. I don't think he'll call me. But

98 percent of my people are for me. They identify with my struggle,

the same one they're fighting every day on the streets. Anybody who thinks Frazier can whup me is an 'Uncle Tom'."

MUHAMMAD ALI before the Frazier fight.
(Budd Schulberg, *Loser and Still Champion*, p.162)

"I'm going to make him quit. No matter what name he goes by, Clay or Ali, *he'll quit.* The fight won't last ten rounds."

JOE FRAZIER before the fight. (*Baltimore Sun*, 3.7.1971)

"He can keep that pretty head; I don't want it.

What I'm going to do is try and pull those kidneys out.

Then I'll be in business. He won't
be able to take it to the body no more.
He'll start snatching his sore body away
and the head will be leaning in.

*That's when I'll take his head, but then
it won't be pretty, or maybe he just won't care."*

JOE FRAZIER, (*Sports Illustrated,* 2.22.1971)

(RIGHT) ALI UNLOADS A RIGHT CROSS BUT FAILS
TO STALL FRAZIER'S RELENTLESS ATTACK.

"Ali's defeat was not mind over matter, but matter over mind. *His body couldn't perform physically the way his mind thought it could.*"

Former light-heavyweight champion, **JOSE TORRES**, a ringside spectator. (*New York Post*, 3.9.1971)

(ABOVE) ALI HEADS FOR THE CANVAS AFTER CATCHING A LEFT HOOK ON THE CHIN IN THE FINAL ROUND. HE BEAT THE COUNT, BUT HE DID NOT NEED THE JUDGES TO TELL HIM THAT HE HAD LOST HIS FIRST ENCOUNTER WITH FRAZIER, SEEN WAVING TO AN APPRECIATIVE CROWD IN NEW YORK (RIGHT).

A JOYOUS FRAZIER IS CONGRATULATED BY TRAINER, YANK DURHAM.

"Just lost a fight, that's all. *I'll probably be a better man for it.*

There are more important things to worry about in life. Presidents get assassinated. Civil rights

leaders get assassinated. The world goes on. I had my day. You lose, you don't shoot yourself."

MUHAMMAD ALI contemplating defeat. (Bob Lipsyte, *Free to Be Muhammad Ali,* p.96)

vs. Jimmy Ellis
July 26, 1971

ASTRODOME, HOUSTON, TEXAS. KO12.

"Fighting Ali was strange after all the good times between us. He introduced me to Angelo Dundee and encouraged me to build my career. When I won the WBA title when he was in exile, he wasn't angry. He was happy for me. When we fought each other, I thought I could beat him. I figured I had the style and speed and his legs weren't the same anymore. The shot I looked for all night was the one he got me with. He came over my jab with a right hand. Afterward, there wasn't any bitterness between us.

I shook his hand and said, 'Hey, you got me.' *And I still love and respect the man."*

JIMMY ELLIS, a boyhood friend of Ali, in retrospect. (Thomas Hauser, *Muhammad Ali: His Life and Times*, p.240)

ALI TOOK LITTLE SYMPATHY ON BOYHOOD FRIEND JIMMY ELLIS BEFORE RECORDING A 12TH-ROUND KNOCK-OUT IN HOUSTON.

BUSTER MATHIS, ONCE DESCRIBED AS A "DANCING ELEPHANT" MANAGED TO SURVIVE THIS KNOCKDOWN IN THE 12TH ROUND AND FINISH HIS FIGHT WITH ALI.

MATHIS '71
vs. Buster Mathis
November 17, 1971

ASTRODOME, HOUSTON, TEXAS. W12.

BLIN '71
vs. Jürgen Blin
December 26, 1971

HALLENSTADOIN ARENA, ZURICH, SWITZERLAND. KO7.

ALI APPEARS TO BE ALL BUSINESS BEFORE HIS FIGHT AGAINST JÜRGEN BLIN IN SWITZERLAND AS PART OF HIS WORLDWIDE TOUR. BLIN, A WEST GERMAN, PROVED NO MATCH IN ONLY LASTING SEVEN ROUNDS.

FOSTER '72
vs. Mac Foster
April 1, 1972

MARTIAL ARTS HALL, TOKYO, JAPAN. W15.

FOSTER, SHOWN TRADING PUNCHES WITH ALI, WAS NO EASY FOIL IN LOSING A 15-ROUND DECISION.

"I was in the Marines, the infantry, for six-and-a-half years and did two tours in Vietnam. I didn't think about boxing until I read Cassius Clay saying **it took more guts to face a 200-pounder in the ring than it does to face a 100-pound machine gun.** Shucks, at least you have an even chance in the ring."

MAC FOSTER, an ex-marine who served in Vietnam, on why he always wanted to fight Ali. (*Washington Post*, 5.6.1970)

ALI CLIMBS INTO THE RING IN TOKYO PREDICTING A FIFTH-ROUND KNOCK-OUT.

SOMETHING CATCHES ALI'S EYE AS HE ENTERS THE ARENA IN TORONTO FOR A REMATCH WITH GEORGE CHUVALO. ONCE AGAIN, THE RUGGED CANADIAN PROVED TO BE ONE OF ALI'S MOST-STUBBORN FOES IN LOSING A 12-ROUND VERDICT.

CHUVALO '72
vs. George Chuvalo
May 1, 1972

PACIFIC COLISEUM, VANCOUVER, CANADA. W12.

QUARRY '72

vs. Jerry Quarry
June 27, 1972

CONVENTION CENTER, LAS VEGAS, NEVADA. KO7.

"I was sharp and ready. *I told the referee to stop it because the man was out on his feet."*

MUHAMMAD ALI after the second fight with Jerry Quarry. (*Baltimore Evening Sun*, 6.28.1972)

MUHAMMAD ALI USES HIS SUPERIOR REACH TO FEND OFF CHARGING JERRY QUARRY IN THEIR REMATCH IN NEVADA.
QUARRY'S IRISH FEATURES WERE AGAIN BADLY BATTERED BEFORE SUCCUMBING IN SEVEN ROUNDS.

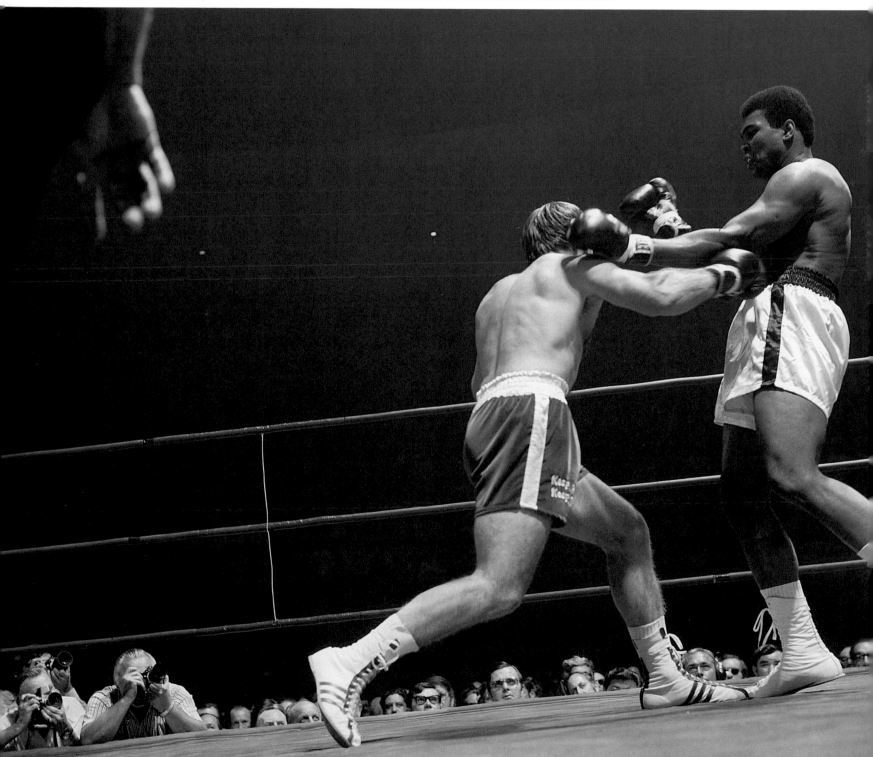

LEWIS '72

vs. Al "Blue" Lewis
July 19, 1972

CROKE PARK, DUBLIN, IRELAND. KO11.

"In 1968, Clay did me a helluva favor.

At the time I had only 11 pro fights, but when he came to Detroit to fight some exhibitions during his exile, he gave me a chance, three rounds at $100 a round. I was fresh out of prison and it gave me a name for myself. I said then, if they ever gave him his license back, I'd go anyplace to help him." AL "BLUE" LEWIS, (*New York Daily News*, 5.9.1972)

RAISING HIS FISTS TO THE SKY, ALI CELEBRATES AFTER STOPPING AL "BLUE" LEWIS IN THE 11TH ROUND OF THE DUBLIN BRAWL.

AN ESTIMATED 7,000 GATE CRASHERS SWELLED ATTENDANCE AT THIS SUMMER SPECTACLE.

A SOMBRE LOOKING ALI TAKES QUESTIONS FROM THE MEDIA BEFORE HIS FIGHT WITH AL "BLUE" LEWIS IN IRELAND. ALI SCORED AN 11TH ROUND TKO.

PATTERSON '72
vs. Floyd Patterson
September 20, 1972.

MADISON SQUARE GARDEN, NEW YORK CITY. KO8

FORMER HEAVYWEIGHT CHAMPION, FLOYD PATTERSON, MAKES CERTAIN TO CHECK ALI'S WEIGHT PRIOR TO
THEIR REMATCH IN NEW YORK. THIS TIME PATTERSON LASTED ONLY SEVEN ROUNDS.

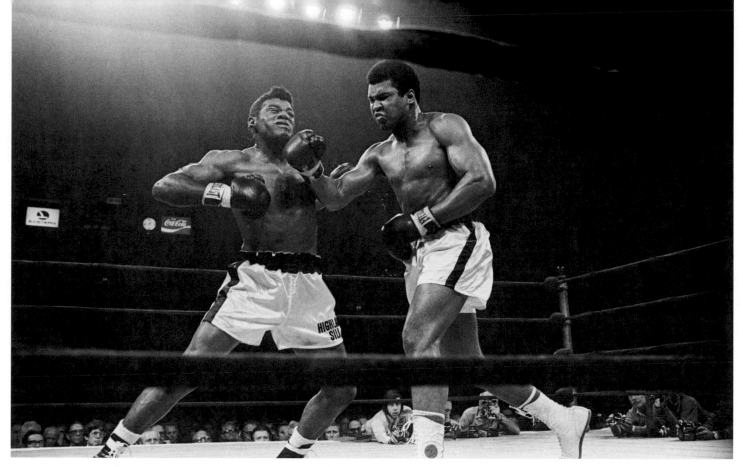

ALTHOUGH NEVER CONSIDERED A BIG PUNCHER, ALI DISPLAYS POWER IN STAGGERING PATTERSON WITH A RIGHT CROSS.

"I personally didn't like the doctor stopping the fight. I thought I was holding my own until the eye closed.

I know Cassius didn't carry me this time . . .
But anytime I'm defeated, I'm ashamed.

There's no more moustache or beard [referring to his disguise after getting
knocked out in one round by Sonny Liston], but I'm still ashamed."

FLOYD PATTERSON, (*Baltimore Sun*, 9.21.1972)

"Because of his age [37], **I thought Patterson would be
finished after two rounds. But he was in superb condition.**
If I'd listened to the press, he would have given me a worse
lickin' in the first five rounds. I didn't knock him out or
TKO him. I just closed his eye."

MUHAMMAD ALI, who once dubbed Patterson "The Washerwoman".
(*Baltimore Sun*, 9.21.1972)

WITH MADISON SQUARE GARDEN BOXING DIRECTOR JOHN CONDON HOLDING
THE MICROPHONE, ALI DISSECTS HIS REPEAT VICTORY OVER PATTERSON.

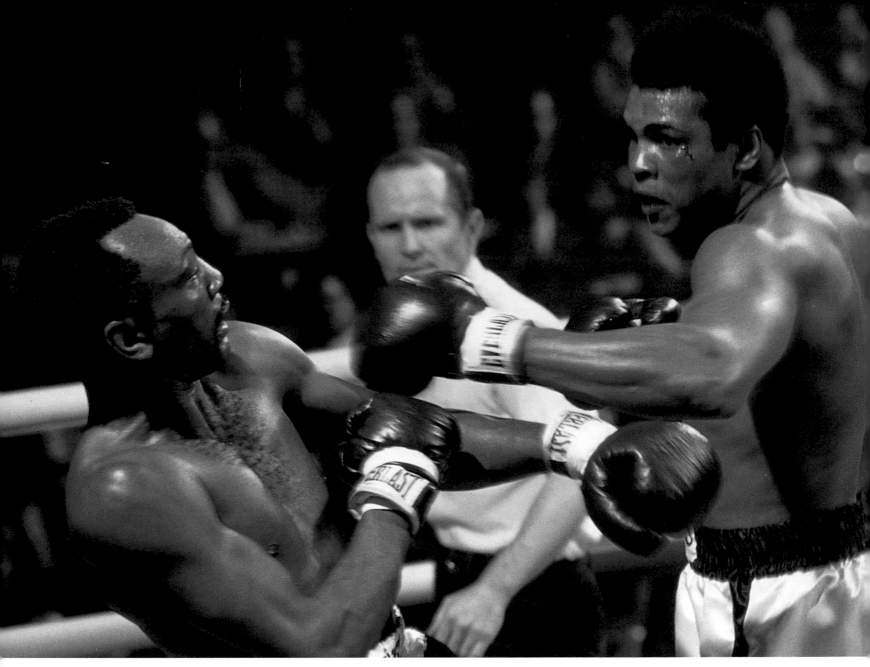

It's Ali on the offensive against light-heavyweight king, Bob Foster, a feared slugger.

FOSTER '72

vs. Bob Foster
November 21, 1972

HIGH SIERRA THEATRE, STATELINE, NEVADA. KO8.

"This proves I'm human.

I've got cut and bruises alongside my left eye and that's something that no other professional

fighter has been able to do to me … Foster gave me trouble all through the fight. I didn't

know a man could land so many left jabs."

MUHAMMAD ALI on the cuts and bruises sustained to his left eye. (*Associated Press*, 11.22.1972)

BUGNER '73

vs. Joe Bugner
February 14, 1973

CONVENTION CENTER, LAS VEGAS, NEVADA. W12.

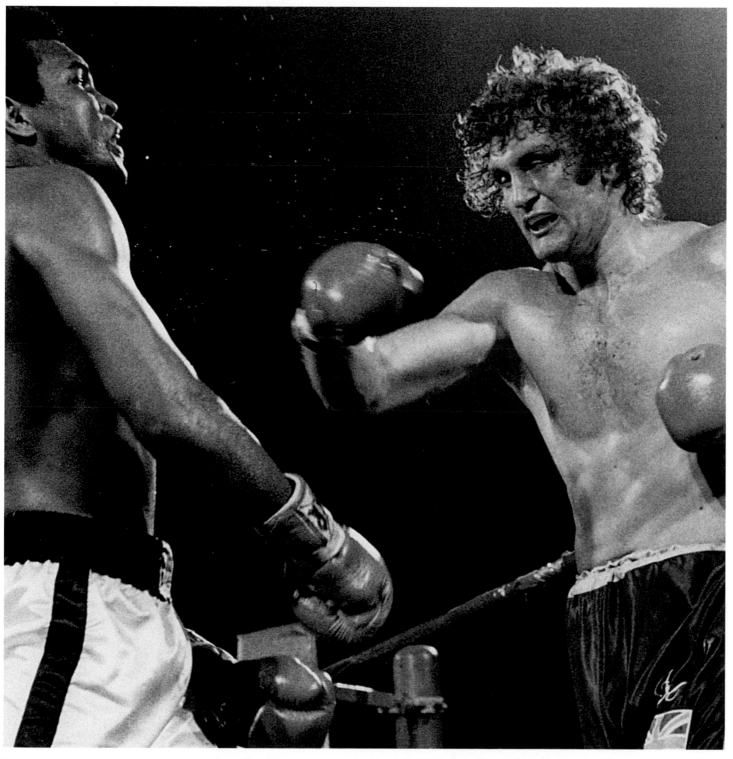

ALI AND JOE BUGNER CLASHED ON VALENTINE'S DAY IN LAS VEGAS, AND IT ALMOST SEEMED LIKE A "LOVE-IN" TO THE CROWD WITNESSING THE SLOW-PACED FIGHT. ALI, SPORTING A BEJEWELLED ROBE PRESENTED TO HIM BY ELVIS PRESLEY, WALKED AWAY WITH A 12-ROUND DECISION—HIS TENTH STRAIGHT VICTORY.

The Broken Jaw

Of the five losses marring Muhammad Ali's professional boxing career, none was more galling or haunting than the one he suffered against a then relatively obscure Ken Norton at the San Diego Sports Arena on March 31, 1973 when the muscular ex-Marine won a split decision and also shattered Ali's jaw.

In fact, for all the celebrity and nostalgia attached to his classic ring trilogy with arch-rival Joe Frazier, Ali experienced a more difficult time trying to solve the free-swinging aggressive style of Norton, blessed with a Tarzan-like physique and a size-13 fist. Like Frazier, Ali would battle Norton three times in a four-year span and there are a goodly number of knowledge-able boxing writers who believe that Norton won all three.

It is hardly a coincidence that renowned trainer, Eddie Futch, who masterminded Norton's stunning upset of Ali, was also an advisor to Frazier when he handed Ali his first defeat in New York two years earlier. Futch, who, in his fighting days as a welterweight, used all his guile to survive sparring sessions in Detroit with heavyweight champion Joe Louis, was a master strategist and unparalleled at finding and exploiting an opponent's weakness.

He became convinced Norton had the style to beat Ali after the two engaged in an impromp-tu meeting at the Hoover Gym in San Diego in 1969 when Ali was still in political exile.

As Futch would recall, "You know, Ali. He's like the Pied Piper. Everywhere he goes there's a crowd following him, and so he decided to show off a bit. He got Ken trapped in a corner and felt he could keep him there while he entertained everybody. I'll never forget it. Ken just picked Ali up beneath his elbows, turned around and set him down in the corner.

"When he did it again, I think it embarrassed Ali. The next round Ali said he was through fooling around and really came after Norton. He threw a big flurry, but Ken nailed him with a hard right. After that, Ali backed off and began clowning again.

"The next day Ali showed up again and began roaring, 'Where's Norton? I'm going to get him today.' I said, 'No, you're not. The next time you get him in the ring it will be for big money.'" [1]

And that is exactly what happened. Norton was guaranteed $50,000, a princely sum con-sidering he had earned only $300 for his previous fight against Charlie Reno.

For $50,000, Norton told Ali's representatives, he would fight the Russian army. In fact, he had seriously considered retiring from boxing following a divorce which left him to support an infant son on his paltry ring earnings.

"I was ready to go back to my hometown in Illinois," Norton said. "I packed all my belong-ings in my car and called my parents. But my mother said, 'If you quit now, you will quit everything you try from now on.'" [2]

Despite his gaudy 24–1 record, everyone viewed Norton as a "tune-up" for Ali who was looking down the road to a rematch with Frazier. Sportscaster Howard Cosell, who had hitched his star to Ali's career, labeled the fight the worst mismatch in history. A few weeks before the fight, promoter Bob Arum called Norton's manager, Bob Biron, and asked in a concerned voice, "Can your guy go more than two rounds? If not, with this fight on national television, we'll look awfully silly." [3]

Ali bought into all the pre-fight hype and trained for less than three weeks. He also managed to sprain his ankle by clowning around on a golf course, revolutionizing the ancient game by hitting the ball on the move.

Said Ali, "I started believing I couldn't be whipped. After losing to Frazier, I'd won a lot of easy fights against 'Blue' Lewis, Henry Cooper, Buster Mathis, Jürgen Blin and Jerry Quarry. I didn't have to train hard and discipline myself in order to win. I learned that too many easy victories can ruin a fighter just like a long line of defeats. You start thinking your name alone will win. You forget all the sacrifices that go into winning." [4]

Norton was not the least bit awed by Ali's reputation. A gifted athlete, he had excelled in football, basketball and track in high school, winning the 100, 220 and discus events in one dual meet. Winning effortlessly was something he learned to expect.

As the showdown with Ali approached, Norton a 5–1 underdog, said confidently, "I respect him for what he stands for. Anyone who defies the government and stands by it, deserves respect. And I respect him as a fighter. But I don't fear him at all. I don't fear any man. There's no room for fear in the ring." [5]

Having Futch in his corner only boosted his confidence. For the veteran trainer had spotted several flaws in Ali's armor that would allow Norton to overcome his rival's superior boxing skills.

As Futch later revealed, "The jab was a big reason Ali never figured out why he had so much trouble with Norton in their three fights … Norton was strong. He was awkward. And he was as tall as Ali. After they met in the gym in 1969, I began thinking how Norton could avoid Ali's strength and exploit his weaknesses.

"I told Ken, 'You're not going to hit Ali by slipping or pulling back, dropping underneath or parrying. You have to hit him when he's punching. When he starts to jab, you punch with him.' That destroyed Ali's rhythm." [6]

But more than any strategy, the fight turned dramatically after Norton caught Ali on the ropes and broke his jaw with a vicious hook. The only question is, when did the crucial blow occur?

Dr. Ferdie Pacheco, who was working Ali's corner, insists it happened early in the fight. "The jaw was broken in the second round," he said. "Ali was missing a tooth at the point of the fracture. And that, plus the pressure of Norton's punch, broke his jaw. I could feel the separation with my fingertips. That's when winning took priority over medical care. When the bell rung, I was no longer a doctor, I was a ring second.

"As a doctor, I should have said, 'Stop the fight!' There's no disgrace in a broken jaw. But Norton was a guy Ali was supposed to beat hands down, and, at that point in his career, Ali couldn't afford a loss.

"Also, there were politics involved. We weren't fighting in a sterile environment. Everything had to do with Muslims, Vietnam and civil rights. You couldn't have a white guy stopping the fight, especially if Ali didn't want it stopped. The pain must have been awful, and he couldn't fight his fight because he was protecting his jaw. And still he fought 12 rounds. God almighty he was tough. Underneath that soft exterior, there was an ugly Teamsters Union trucker at work." [7]

Futch disagrees with Pacheco. He believes the jaw was broken in the closing rounds. "Ali's best round in the fight was the 11th. And he came out strong in the 12th until Ken smashed his jaw. Ali covered up the rest of the round, not fighting at all." [8]

Early or late, Ali could not overcome the injury and offered no excuses in losing to an unheralded rival. "I took a nobody and made him a monster," he said ruefully. [9]

After the fight, Ali was rushed to the hospital, underwent a 90-minute operation and had his jaw wired shut. Norton had accomplished a feat no one before or after him had managed—silencing Ali.

"That was the worst punishment of all," a vanquished Ali would later lament. [10]

NORTON '73

vs. Ken Norton
March 31, 1973

SPORTS ARENA, SAN DIEGO, CALIFORNIA. L12.

"I wanted to stop it in the second round but Ali wouldn't let me.

The commission doctor told me he had a broken jaw."

Trainer **ANGELO DUNDEE** on Ali's broken jaw. (*Associated Press*, 4.1.1973)

LIGHTLY-REGARDED KEN NORTON BECAME AN INSTANT CELEBRITY AFTER HIS SHOCKING 12-ROUND VICTORY OVER HEAVILY-FANCIED ALI IN SAN DIEGO.

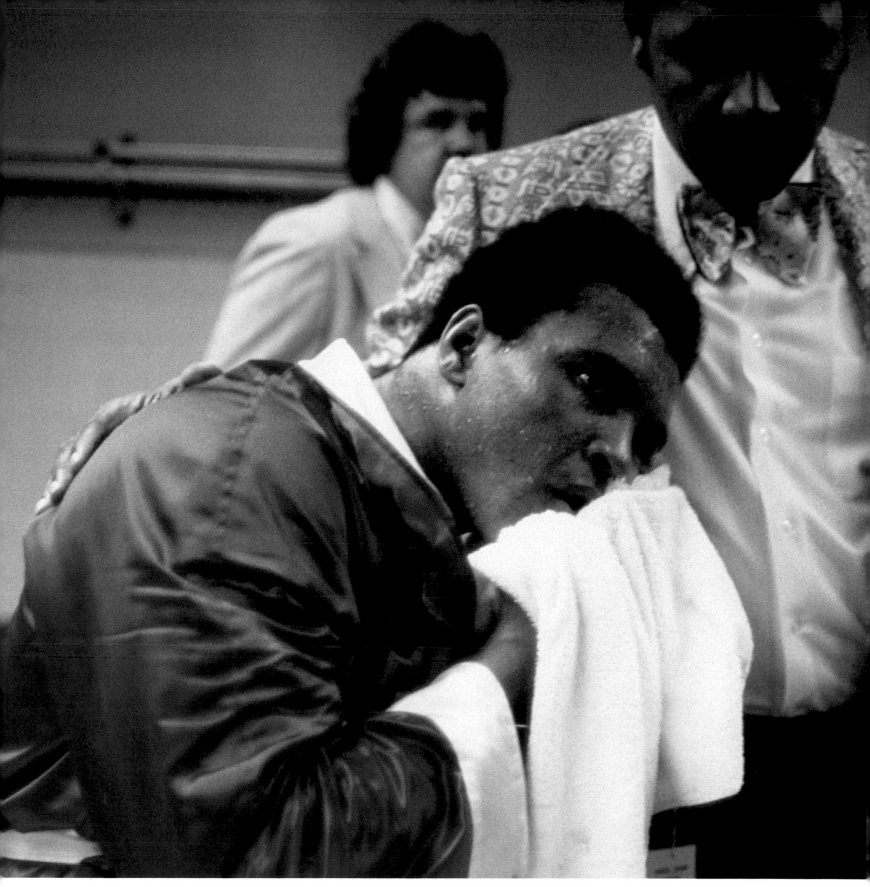

A CONCERNED DON KING LOOKS ON AS ALI APPLIES ICE TO HIS BROKEN JAW AFTER DEFEAT BY KEN NORTON.

"I know I broke his jaw.

I think it was in the first round. I don't know what punch did it … My plan was to keep pressure on the man, keep him moving and get him tired. I was never hurt, but he stung me with a right once. In my mind, I won all the way" KEN NORTON, (*Associated Press*, 4.1.1973)

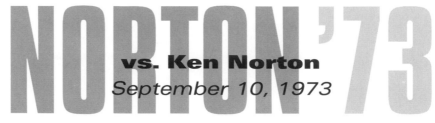

NORTON '73

vs. Ken Norton
September 10, 1973

FORUM, INGLEWOOD, CALIFORNIA. W12.

(BELOW) A SMIRKING ALI POINTS TO THE JAW KEN NORTON SHATTERED IN THEIR FIRST ENCOUNTER. IT HEALED QUICK ENOUGH TO GIVE ALI A CHANCE FOR REVENGE SIX MONTHS LATER IN LOS ANGELES—ALI EMERGED WITH A 12-ROUND DECISION AND KEPT HIS CHIN INTACT. (RIGHT) KEN NORTON, WHO HAD LONG-TIME ALI NEMESIS EDDIE FUTCH IN HIS CORNER, HAD AN AWKWARD STYLE THAT CONFUSED ALI. ALTHOUGH THE JUDGES FAVORED ALI, NORTON SHOWS HE HAD LITTLE TROUBLE PENETRATING HIS DEFENSE.

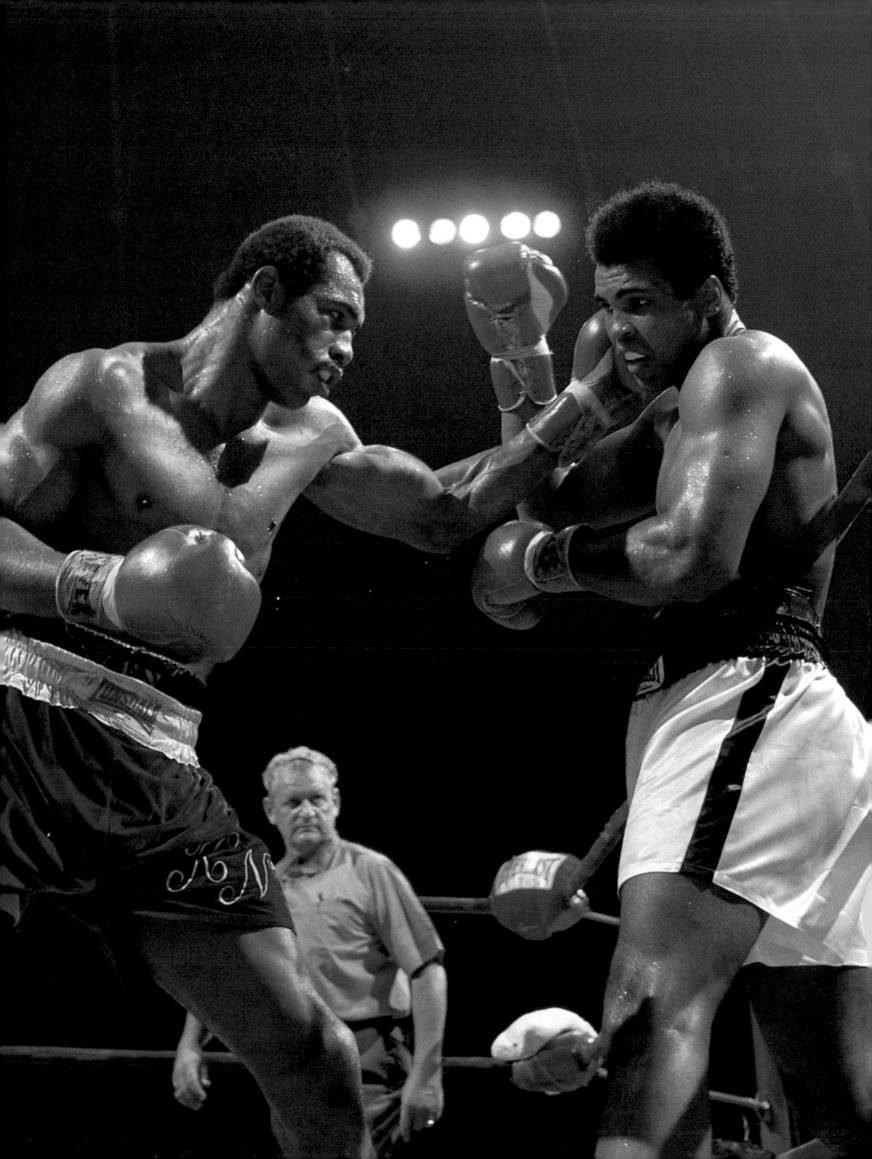

ALI STRIKES A MENACING POSE PRIOR TO HIS FIGHT WITH RUDI LUBBERS IN INDONESIA. LUBBERS PROVED A DURABLE FOE, LASTING 12 ROUNDS AND HELPING ALI TO GET IN SHAPE FOR HIS SECOND MATCH WITH JOE FRAZIER.

LUBBERS '73

vs. Rudi Lubbers
October 20, 1973

SENYAN STADIUM, DJAKARTA, INDONESIA. W12.

"Lubbers is a good fighter. I hit him with everything I could."

MUHAMMAD ALI, (*Associated Press*, 10.21.1973)

"I'm saving it for Joe Frazier."

MUHAMMAD ALI when asked why he seldom threw a right against Lubbers. (*Associated Press*, 10.21.1973)

vs. Joe Frazier
January 28, 1974

MADISON SQUARE GARDEN, NEW YORK CITY. W12.

"Joe was much better than I thought. You can't take nothing from him. He took it and had me in trouble.

He had me out on my feet twice."

MUHAMMAD ALI, (*Baltimore Sun*, 1.29.1974)

JOE FRAZIER GETS A RARE OPPORTUNITY TO STEAL THE MICROPHONE FROM ALI AT THE PRESS CONFERENCE ANNOUNCING THEIR REMATCH IN NEW YORK. MADISON SQUARE GARDEN BOXING DIRECTOR, JOHN CONDON, ACTS AS MODERATOR.

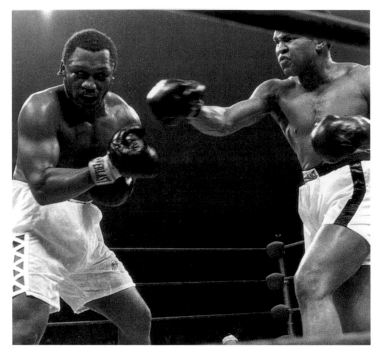

ALI UNLEASHES A STRAIGHT RIGHT AS JOE FRAZIER TAKES COVER.

"It wasn't the first and for damn sure wouldn't be the last time Clay got a gift from the judges.

Norton was robbed five months earlier, now me … But I didn't make a big fuss about the decision. That wasn't my way. I was no crybaby like Clay after the first one, talking his bullshit and trying to persuade folks he didn't get his ass kicked. In boxing, you take the good with the bad, and push on."

JOE FRAZIER, (Joe Frazier with Phil Berger, *Smokin' Joe*, p.148)

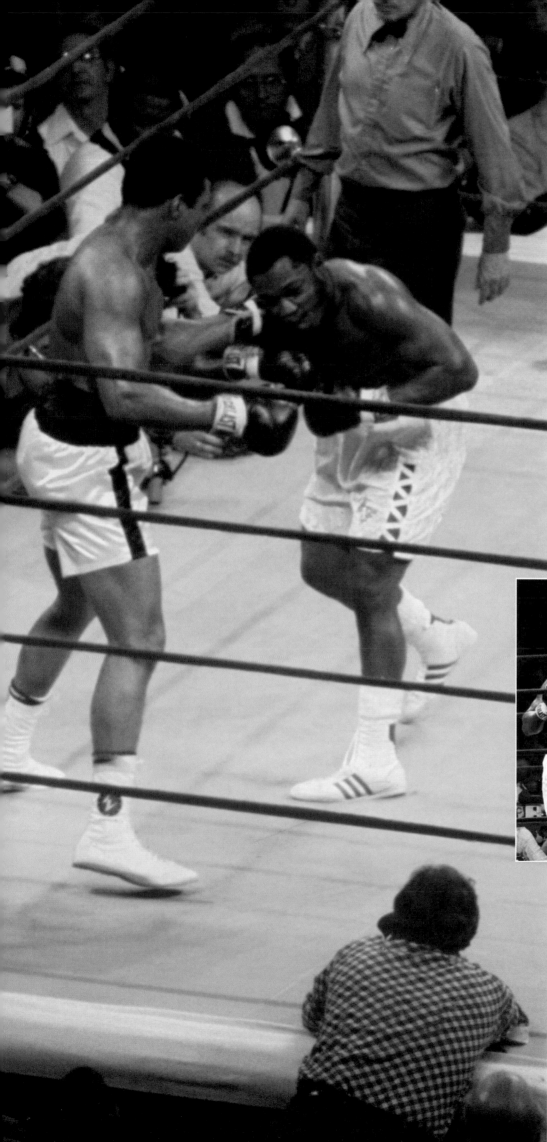

I think we should do it again. I'm not gonna duck Joe. I'll give him all the chances he wants."

MUHAMMAD ALI,
(*Baltimore Sun*, 1.29.1974)

JOE FRAZIER AND ALI EXCHANGE PUNCHES (ABOVE), BUT ALI (LEFT) SEEMS TO BE GETTING THE BETTER OF IT AND WON THE JUDGES' APPROVAL.

Zaire, Manila and Beyond

SIX

I n the millions of words and tomes commemorating Muhammad Ali's inspirational "Rumble in the Jungle" with George Foreman, a salient fact often overlooked was that the heavyweight championship fight originally scheduled in Kinsasha, Zaire, on September 25, 1974, was postponed for six weeks after Foreman sustained an eye injury in training.

Psychologically, this proved a devastating blow to Foreman, who felt he had become a political prisoner of Zaire dictator, Mobutu Sese Seko, who had guaranteed the two fighters a record $10 million for the privilege of becoming the first country to sponsor a major boxing match.

As Foreman would recall in his autobiography, "I was miserable in Zaire. My first quarters were at an old army base infested with rats, lizards and insects. Surrounded by cyclone fencing and barbed wire, it was patrolled and inhabited by rowdy soldiers.

"This was clearly Muhammad Ali country. Sentiment in his favor colored how everyone looked at me. Most people wanted him to win back the title as much as he did. As far as he was concerned, I held the championship taken away from him when he refused to be drafted into the Army. And who was I? The goof who waved the American flag after winning an Olympic gold medal. If I knocked him out, the most I'd get would be grudging respect for vanquishing a legend. And if I lost, there'd be a big crowd at the station, jeering me back to Pallookaville." [1]

Foreman was not alone in sharing this perception. Leon Gast, who produced the Oscar-winning documentary, *When We Were Kings*, said, "A lot of people say it was the biggest psyche job ever. Ali stayed in Zaire and actually enjoyed the time he was there. Foreman, on the other hand, was miserable from the day he arrived. He wanted to get in, end the fight, and get out. Then he had to stay an extra six weeks.

"The fight meant so much to Africans," added Gast, "because there had never been a cultural event that focused so much attention on them. Ali was attuned to that; Foreman wasn't. Both fighters kept saying, 'From slave ship to championship,' but when Ali said it, you knew it was more than just hype." [2]

While Foreman glowered and grumbled, Ali seized on the fight's postponement to capture the hearts and souls of Zaireans and turn them into a weapon against the sullen champion. "These are my people, and I ain't leaving," [3] said Ali when rumors spread that both fighters might leave Africa. By fight night, a whole country was in his corner.

Still, a vast majority of ring experts envisioned the fight as a suicide mission for Ali, then 32, and having exhibited signs of slippage in splitting two fights with Ken Norton. Conversely, Foreman, 26, was considered as invincible as role model Sonny Liston was before being exposed by a youthful Ali.

As evidence, Foreman had needed only two rounds to destroy Norton and Joe Frazier, who both held victories over Ali. In the three years prior to meeting Ali, no one had survived more than three rounds against the powerful Texan, unbeaten and scarcely threatened in 40 professional fights.

Norman Mailer, who would write an entire book about the epic brawl, said, "I think Ali was very scared as he got closer to the fight. With his ego, he could keep telling himself that he would dominate Foreman, that he would dance and make a fool of him. But, in his private moments, he had not done nearly as well against Frazier and Norton whom Foreman had demolished." [4]

This view was shared by *New York Times* columnist, Dave Anderson, who wrote, "Foreman might be the heaviest puncher in the history of the heavyweight division. For a few rounds, Ali might be able to escape Foreman's sledgehammer strength, but not for 15 rounds, and for the first time in his career, Ali will be counted out. That could happen in the first round." [5]

The only chance given to Ali to survive against this 6' 3", 220-pound dreadnought, was to use his superior speed and boxing ability. Ali, himself, had come to the same conclusion. But his advanced boxing age, coupled with the extreme humidity in the arena when the pre-dawn battle began, inspired him to adopt the "Rope-A-Dope" defensive strategy that would ultimately prove a stroke of genius.

As Ali would confess to biographer Thomas Hauser, "I didn't really plan what happened that night. But when a fighter gets into the ring, he has to adjust to the conditions. Against George, the ring was slow. Dancing all night, my legs would have got tired.

"So, after the first round, I decided to do what I did in training when I got tired. I figured I'd be able to handle George off the ropes early in the fight when I was fresh. I gave George what he thought he wanted. He hit hard, and a couple of times, he shook me bad. But I blocked and dodged most of what he threw, and each round his punches got slower and hurt less." [6]

Ali's corner was as befuddled by the strategy as Foreman, most of all veteran trainer, Angelo Dundee, who kept beseeching Ali to hit and run.

"I won't kid you," said Dundee. "When he went to the ropes, I felt sick. Going into the fight, I thought Muhammad would win, but not that way.

"I saw him dancing for five or six rounds. Then I imagined him picking up the pace when George got tired and knocking him out in the late rounds, but everything planned was around not getting hit. Muhammad was going to stay on his toes, show George all kinds of angles. That shows what I know. It was a great fight, and I had a hell of a seat to watch it." [7]

Continuing to ignore his corner's advice, Ali occasionally emerged from his protective cocoon to catch Foreman with a sharp jab or counter punch. By the sixth round, it was evident that Foreman's relentless bludgeoning of Ali's arms and shoulders had brought on utter fatigue. As Wilfrid Sheed observed, "There's a saying in boxing that if any fighter has to go 15 rounds with the heavy punching bag, the bag would win. George went eight." [8]

Ali had done the impossible, finishing Foreman with a right hand flush on the chin and bringing a deafening roar of approval from the 60,000-odd spectators who had chanted "*Ali, bombaye*" (Ali, kill him) throughout the fight.

A distraught Foreman would later offer a litany of excuses for his stunning defeat. He said he wasn't given sufficient time to regain his conditioning following his eye injury, claimed his drinking water had been drugged, accused Dundee of tampering with the ropes, and, finally, said he had been victimized by a fast ten count by referee, Zack Clayton.

As the years passed, he grudgingly accepted the fact that he had simply been outsmarted. "I'll admit it, he outthought me; he outfought me," said Foreman, whose image had changed to a smiling, joking Madison avenue huckster. "That night, he was just the better man in the ring … Finally, I realized I'd lost to a great champion—probably the greatest of them all— and now I'm just proud to be part of the Ali legend." [9]

Truly, Ali had become a legend. No athletic contest in history had so captivated the public's imagination. Toppling Foreman would prove to be the crowning moment of his storied career. His latest miracle had silenced his few remaining critics and become much more than heavyweight champion a second time. He was now "King of the World".

"Mr. President, I've been a citizen of the United States
of America for 33 years
and was never invited to the White House.
It sure gives me pleasure to be invited to the Black House."

Muhammad Ali, on meeting President Mobutu at a reception in his honor at the presidential palace in Kinshasa.

(*The Good, The Bad and the Ugly*)

STROLLING THROUGH THE STREETS OF KINSHASA, ALI SHOWED HE WAS CLEARLY THE FAVORITE OF
THE ZAIRE POPULACE IN HIS HERALDED MATCH WITH THEN-UNBEATEN GEORGE FOREMAN.

FOREMAN '74

vs. George Foreman
October 30, 1974

20TH OF MAY STADIUM, KINSHASA, ZAIRE. KO8. (REGAINED WORLD HEAVYWEIGHT TITLE)

"It's a great feeling being in a country operated by black people. I wish all black people in America could see this. In America, we've been led to believe we can't do without the white man and all we know about Africa is jungles, a bunch of natives leading white men on a safari, and maybe one of the white men is trapped by a gorilla and the natives save him. We never get shown African cars, boats or jet planes or the African television stations. Everything here is black—the soldiers, the President, the face on the money. It don't seem possible, but 28 million people run this country and not one white man is involved.

I used to think Africans were savages. But now that I'm here, I've learned many Africans are wiser than we are. They speak English and two or three other languages. Ain't that something? *We in America are the savages.*"

MUHAMMAD ALI after arriving in Zaire. (Howard Bingham tape collection)

After spending the better part of the fight on the ropes fending off Foreman's sledgehammer blows, Ali springs to the attack and staggers the champion with a booming right hand.

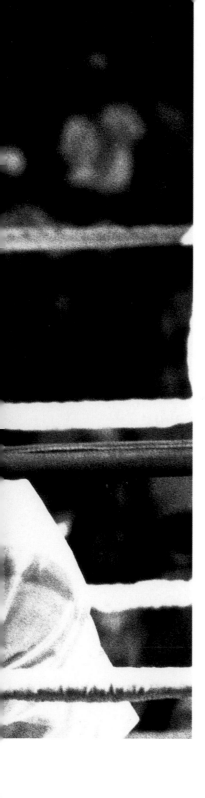

Foreman sends Ali's head flying with a long right during the relentless barrage of the early rounds.

"I'm the only black man in the world standin' up for my people.

All the rednecks and Uncle Toms
are pulling for me to lose.
I'm gonna whup George Foreman,
not for the money, not so
I can have a blonde on both arms—
but so I can go with blacks,
use it to practice what Elijah
[Muhammad] teaches."

MUHAMMAD ALI before the fight. (*Louisville Journal-Courier*, 9.15.1978)

"Muhammad amazed me; I'll admit it. He outthought me, he outfought me. Before the fight, I thought I'd knock him out easy— one or two rounds. And what I remember about the fight is that **I went out and hit Muhummad with the hardest body shot I ever delivered to an opponent.** *Anybody else in the world would have crumbled.*

Muhammad cringed. I could see he was hurt. But he had that look in his eyes, like he was saying I'm not going to let you hurt me …

Everything else happened too quick. I got burned out …

I was the aggressor. There was no doubt about that, *but I knew in some way I was losing."*

GEORGE FOREMAN in retrospect. (Thomas Hauser, *Muhammad Ali, His Life and Times,* p.278)

DESPITE HIS CORNER'S ADMONITIONS, ALI CONTINUED TO FIGHT OFF THE ROPES, CATCHING A VICIOUS BODY PUNCH BY FOREMAN.

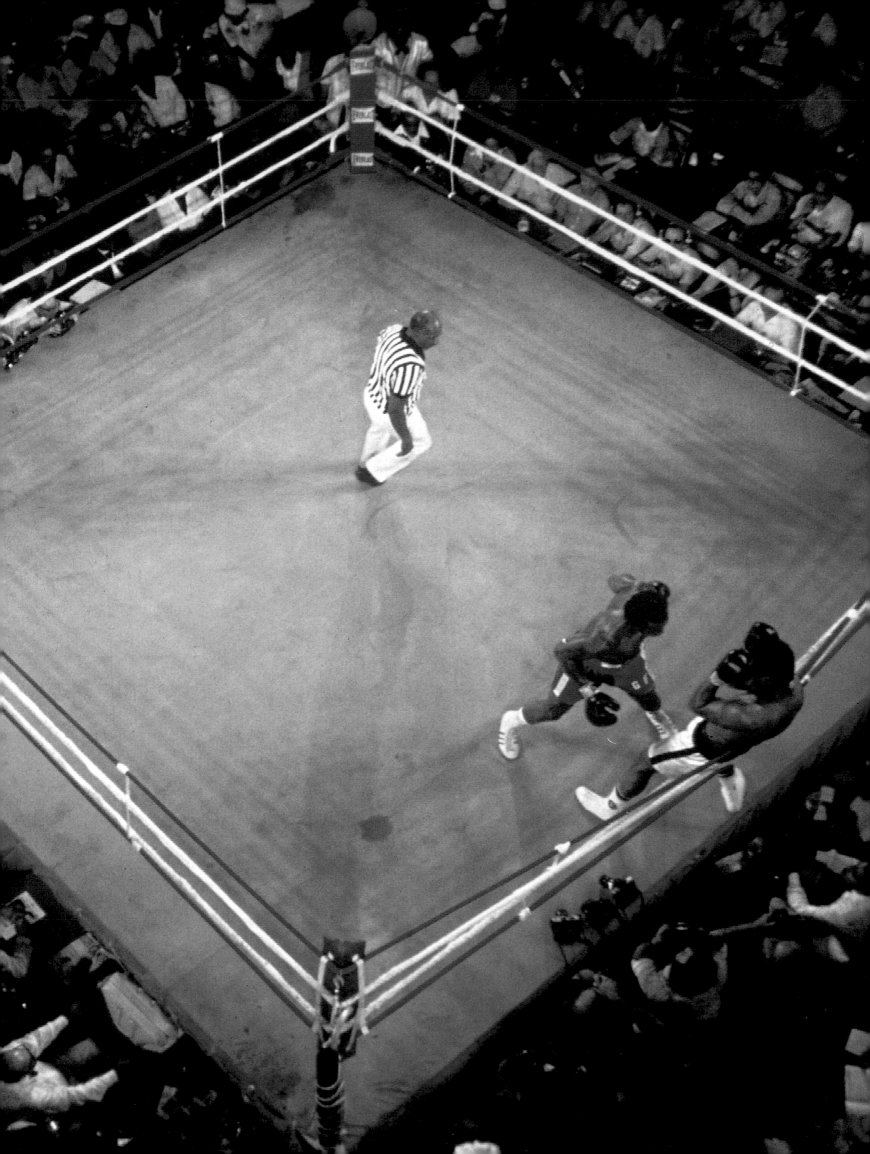

"I didn't really plan
what happened that night.
A fighter has to adjust according to the conditions he faces.

Against George, the ring was slow. Dancing all night, my legs would have got tired …
I figured I'd be able to handle George off the ropes early in the fight, and if he hit too hard,
I'd start dancing again. George was trapped because attacking was all he knew how to do.

(ABOVE) GEORGE FOREMAN IS HEADED FOR A FALL AFTER
CATCHING A PUNISHING RIGHT FROM ALI.

(LEFT) ALI'S "ROPE-A-DOPE" TACTICS AGAINST HEAVY-PUNCHING GEORGE FOREMAN BECAME
PART OF BOXING FOLKLORE. ALI INSISTED HE ADOPTED THIS UNORTHODOX BATTLE PLAN ONLY
TO GUARD AGAINST FATIGUE THAT WOULD HAVE ENSUED HAD HE BEEN FORCED TO DANCE AND
BOX OUT OF HARM'S WAY ON A SLOW RING.

The punch I knocked him down with,
**if I'd hit him with that in the first round,
he would have gotten up.** But by the time
I got him, he was too exhausted."

MUHAMMAD ALI on the "Rope-A-Dope" strategy.
(Thomas Hauser, *Muhammad Ali, His Life and Times*, p.277)

"'In the seventh round, Muhammad noticed

I was getting tired, that my shots weren't hurting

as much. He said,

'C'mon, George, show me something. *Is that all you got?*

In the eighth, when he neared the ropes,

I began pummeling him again.

He was knocked backward near the corner,

then bounced to the side. Off balance,

I turned to follow him and leaned to follow him

when he threw a left-right combination.

It struck ground zero on my chin.

I remember thinking,

'Boy, I'm going down.'

Muhammad, I'm sure, was as surprised as I was."

GEORGE FOREMAN,

(George Foreman with Joel Engel, *By George*, p.114)

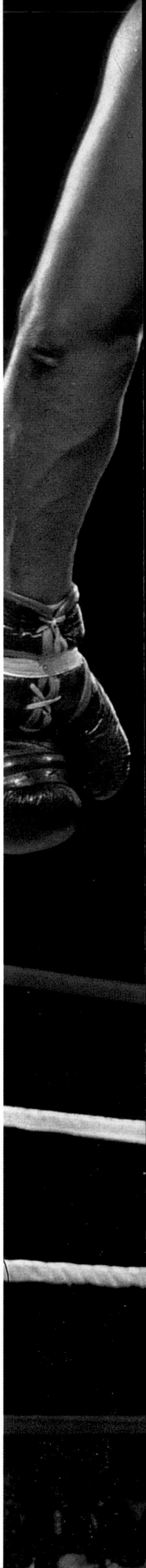

REFEREE ZACK CLAYTON COUNTS
"TEN" OVER GEORGE FOREMAN WHILE
MUHAMMAD ALI OBSERVES HIS HANDI-
WORK. FOREMAN WOULD LATER ACCUSE
CLAYTON OF A "QUICK COUNT" IN
ABSORBING HIS FIRST DEFEAT AND LOSS
OF HIS HEAVYWEIGHT CROWN.

WEPNER '75

vs. Chuck Wepner
March 24, 1975

COLISEUM, CLEVELAND, OHIO. KO15. (RETAINED WORLD HEAVYWEIGHT TITLE)

"In the ninth round, I knocked him down. That was the high point for me. After the round, I felt great. I said, **'Look, I knocked Ali down.'** *And my manager said,* 'Yeah, but he looks pissed.' Ali wasn't really hurt. He came back from the knockdown with four- and five-punch combinations. The last five rounds, I was totally exhausted. The referee, Tony Perez, stopped it in the 15th. I complained, but it wasn't any use. But the record book shows Chuck Wepner took Ali into the 15th round."

CHUCK WEPNER, (Thomas Hauser, *Muhammad Ali, His Life and Times*, p.298)

CHUCK WEPNER, A JOURNEYMAN FIGHTER WHO BECAME A ROLE MODEL FOR SYLVESTER STALLONE'S "ROCKY" CHARACTER, MANAGED TO GO INTO THE FINAL ROUND BEFORE ALI FINALLY STOPPED HIM IN THEIR CLEVELAND MATCH.

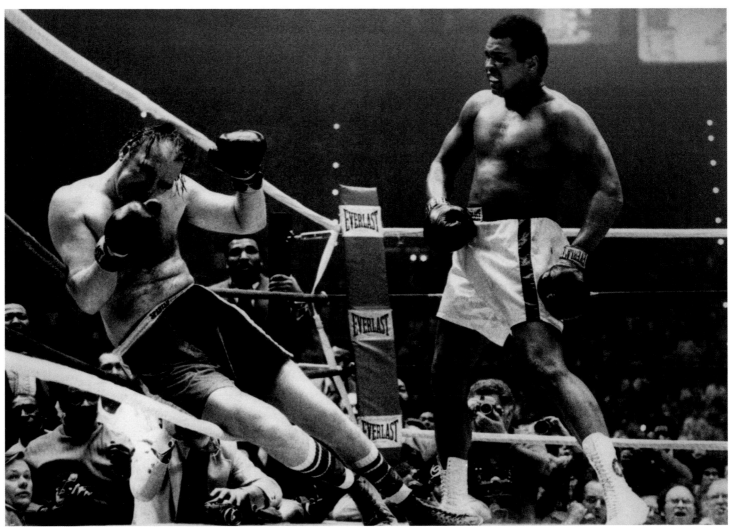

"It was like a mirage—like someone in the desert thinking they can see water and only finding sand."

MUHAMMAD ALI, on again employing "Rope-A-Dope" tactics against Lyle and then suddenly switching to fighting in mid-ring. (*Associated Press*, 5.17.1975)

LYLE '75
vs. Ron Lyle
May 16, 1975

CONVENTION CENTER, LAS VEGAS, NEVADA. KO11.
(RETAINED WORLD HEAVYWEIGHT TITLE)

ALI (ABOVE) SCORES WITH A LONG RIGHT AGAINST RON LYLE. HIS REMATCH WITH BUGNER IN KUALA LUMPUR (BELOW) EARNED HIM $2 MILLION.

BUGNER '75
vs. Joe Bugner
June 30, 1975

MERDEKA STADIUM, KUALA LUMPUR, MALAYSIA. W15.

(RETAINED WORLD HEAVYWEIGHT TITLE)

"I tried to use moving tactics for the first eight rounds and then step up the pace. During the fight Ali kept saying, **'I've got you,'** And I kept answering him, **'No you haven't, baby.'"**

JOE BUGNER after the second of his fights with Muhammad Ali. (*Associated Press*, 6.1.1975)

The Thrilla in Manilla

Ali-Frazier III, a.k.a "The Thrilla in Manila", was one of those exceptional sporting events that lived up to its hype. In later years, it would serve as a measuring stick for all the heavyweight championship fights to follow, but few, if any, would match it for intensity and drama.

Their first fight in 1971 at New York's Madison Square Garden, pitting two unbeaten heavyweights, is remembered more as a "coming out party" for Ali after spending more than three years in political exile. He would suffer the dual embarrassment of being knocked down in the final round and also suffering his first professional loss.

Their second encounter three years later in New York was more or less a private affair with no title at stake and Ali evening the score by winning a unanimous, but unspectacular, decision.

By the time these arch-rivals met for the third and last time in Quezon City outside Manila on October 1, 1975, Ali had recaptured his heavyweight crown and worldwide acclaim for destroying the Foreman myth. Ali would receive $6 million, double Frazier's guarantee. But as John Schulian wrote for *GQ*, "It was never about money or a championship or any of the other things for which men beat one another senseless. Something far more personal was at work. It was as though, as someone once said, Ali and Frazier were fighting for 'the championship of each other'." [1]

In their first two fights, Ali had portrayed Frazier as an "Uncle Tom" controlled by a cartel of white businessmen. Now he stepped up his mean-spirited attack, labeling Frazier as "a gorilla" and illiterate. Ali would later contend he was simply playing mind games and trying to generate ticket sales.

But Frazier took every insult to heart. In his autobiography, he said, "This was Ali's gimmick for the third fight. He'd made me out as a white man for the first two, and now he was gonna make me a cartoon of a nigger, a knuckle-scraping baboon-man. The news guys couldn't resist it. Most of them presented it as a big joke, but they reported it to the world. It wasn't any joke to my children who came home crying from school when classmates teased them that their father was a gorilla." [2]

The genuine animosity Frazier held for Ali was only one angle to this ring spectacle that had a number of subplots, with news of Ali's marital infidelity all but overshadowing the fight itself.

At the time, he was married to Belinda Ali, who, unlike his first wife, Sonji, was a Muslim who followed the sect's strict religious creed. But Ali's ever-roving eye had spied the breathtakingly beautiful Veronica Porsche, one of several attractive women who had been hired by promoter, Don King, to travel with the fighters during a press tour through America. Ali was immediately smitten and his marriage placed in jeopardy.

Things came to a boil at the opulent presidential palace in Manila where Ali and Frazier were the honored guests of the royal family, Ferdinand and Imelda Marcos. Ali was escorted by Veronica and Marcos, when introduced, said, "You have a beautiful wife." Ali failed to correct him, which would be duly noted by a newsman on the scene.

In a *Newsweek* article entitled "The Ali Mystique", Pete Bonventre wrote, "Solemn Muslim guards have given way to streetwise hustlers. Liberals who cherished him as a symbol of pro-black, anti-war attitudes have been replaced by wry connoisseurs of pure showmanship. Even Ali's women, usually black and beautiful, have now been brought out of the back rooms of his life and openly flaunted. As of last week, Belinda was still at home in Chicago, and the stunning Veronica Porsche, sometime known as 'Ali's other wife', was touring Manila with the champ." [3]

This sensational article forced Ali to call a press conference offering an apology to Belinda. Taking the offensive, he said, "Anybody who worries about who's my wife, tell them, you don't worry who I sleep with and I won't worry who you sleep with … They got me on the draft. They got me on religion. But they shouldn't be able to get me for having a girlfriend. The only person I answer to is Belinda Ali, and I don't worry about her." [4]

His lack of concern proved premature. Belinda Ali caught the first plane to Manila and, according to a number of sources, physically attacked her husband during a fiery confrontation before heading back to Chicago the same day, knowing their marriage was over.

Despite this unsettling episode, Ali remained amazingly focused for his heralded fight that began in the late morning and unfolded like a three-act play. The champion would control the early rounds by holding Frazier at bay with a stiff jab and several hard combinations. A notoriously slow starter, Frazier changed the momentum in the middle rounds as he began to catch Ali with solid left hooks. Ali shook his head in derision, and challenged Frazier to continue his assault.

But as former light-heavyweight king Joe Torres would note, "A fighter lies a lot. What is a feint other than a lie. But Frazier is a fighter you can't lie to. He is a computerized machine which has only been fed a truth chart. You can't lie to a machine. You can't fool it with your feints." [5]

Between the tenth and 11th rounds, a fatigued Ali would confide to trainer Angelo Dundee, "This is the closest I've come to dying." But Ali, as he had done so often in the past, called upon his indomitable will to gain renewed strength.

In the 13th round, he would unleash a barrage of unanswered punches that sent Frazier reeling around the ring. A left hook sent Frazier's mouthpiece flying into the crowd. It continued in the 14th as Frazier, his right eye all but swollen shut, could no longer see the punches coming and had only a ghost-like vision of his tormentor.

Like a true warrior, he preferred to be carried out on his shield, but Eddie Futch, his compassionate trainer, took charge before the bell for the final round sounded. "It's all over," he said. "You've taken enough punishment. But no one will ever forget what you did today." [6]

Ali, who had expended all his energy, collapsed in his corner after discovering that Frazier had surrendered. Said Dundee, "Was I worried in Manila? You bet I was; it was a brutal fight. Both guys ran out of gas, only my guy had an extra tank." [7]

In the aftermath, Ali publicly apologized to Frazier, telling his son, Marvis, who would follow his father into the ring, "Tell your father that all the stuff I said about him, I didn't mean it. Your father's a helluva man. I couldn't have taken the punches he took today." [8]

Frazier, in return, offered grudging respect. "We were gladiators. I didn't ask no favors of him, and he didn't ask none of me. I don't like him, but I got to say, in the ring, he was a man." [9]

The classic Ali-Frazier trilogy had ended on an exhilarating note. Realizing the physical toll his victory had taken, Ali grabbed the microphone and told his worldwide audience, "I want to retire. This is too painful, this is too much work."

Indeed, it would have been a perfect way for Ali to lower the curtain and to hear the applause ringing in his ear. But true to his professional code, he would not go quietly into the night. There were still more battles to be fought.

Ali: *"Superman don't need no seat belt."*
Stewardess: "Superman don't need no plane, either."

MUHAMMAD ALI, flying to Manila, responds to stewardess telling him to fasten his seatbelt.

"It will be a killa and a thrilla and a chilla when I get the 'Gorilla' in Manila."

MUHAMMAD ALI

ALI APPEARS TO BE ON THE CAMPAIGN TRAIL PRIOR TO HIS THIRD AND FINAL MEETING WITH JOE FRAZIER IN MANILA.

"Joe and I, *we've paid all the dues we're ever going to pay each other.*"

MUHAMMAD ALI, (*Associated Press*, 10.2.1975)

ALI AND FRAZIER, TWO PROUD WARRIORS WELL BEYOND THEIR FIGHTING PEAK,
LET IT ALL HANG OUT IN THEIR FINAL SHOWDOWN WHICH NOW SERVES AS A
MEASURING STICK FOR HEAVYWEIGHTS.

FRAZIER TAKES A RARE DEFENSIVE STANCE AS ALI TURNS UP THE PRESSURE.

"That was the closest thing to death.

Frazier hit me with body punches that made me want to quit."

MUHAMMAD ALI after the fight. (*Associated Press*, 10.2.1975)

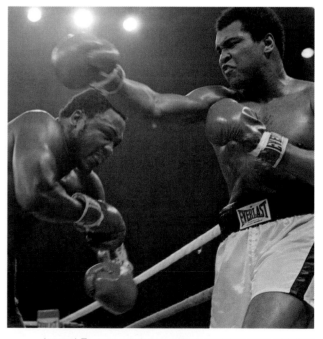

(ABOVE) FRAZIER WAS EXPERIENCING VISION PROBLEMS TRYING
TO WARD OFF ALI'S PUNCHES. (RIGHT) NO LONGER ABLE TO
PRANCE AND DANCE, ALI CONVINCED FRAZIER HE HAD THE
COURAGE OF A LION IN WINNING THIS WAR OF ATTRITION.

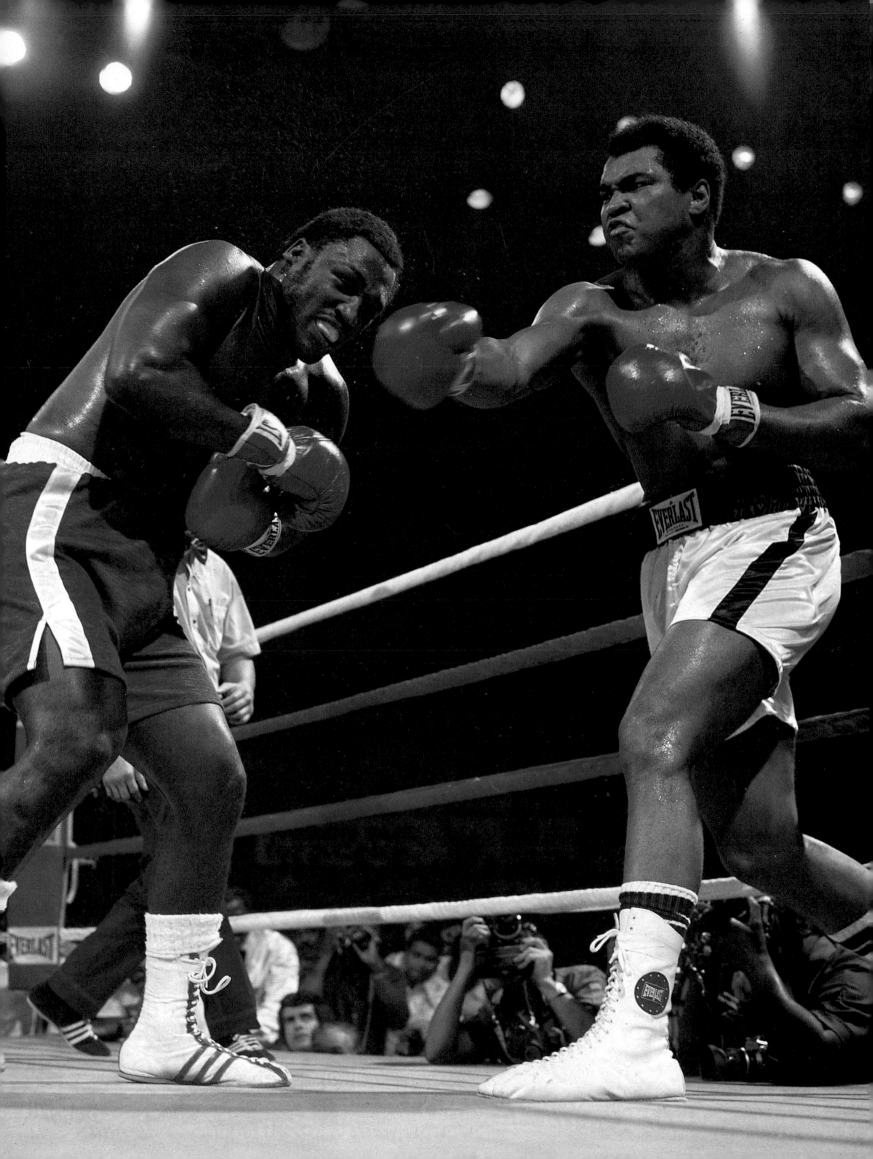

THE END IS NEAR FOR THE GALLANT JOE FRAZIER AS ALI GETS READY TO UNLEASH A WICKED LEFT HOOK IN THE 14TH ROUND.
FRAZIER'S TRAINER, EDDIE FUTCH, WOULD NOT ALLOW HIM TO COME OUT OF THE CORNER FOR THE FINAL ROUND.

"You know, Muhammad was a much better puncher than people gave him credit for.

And Muhammad was always at his best when he felt he had something to prove.

So was I worried in Manila? You bet I was.

It was a brutal fight,

and when it was over, both guys had run out of gas, only my guy had an extra tank."

ANGELO DUNDEE, (Thomas Hauser, *Muhammad Ali, His Life and Times*, p.322)

SURROUNDED BY BROTHER RAHAMAN AND PROMOTER DON KING, ALI DESCRIBES HOW
HE WON THE "RUBBER" MATCH WITH FRAZIER.

"I don't think two big men ever fought fights like me and Joe Frazier.

One fight, maybe. But three times, we were the only ones.

Of all the men I fought, Liston was the scariest, Foreman the most

powerful, Patterson the most skillful. But **the toughest was**
Frazier. He brought out the best
in me, and the best fight we fought was in Manila. That fight, I could

feel something happening to me. God blessed me that day. It was like I

took myself so far and God took me the rest of the way."

MUHAMMAD ALI in retrospect. (Thomas Hauser,
Muhammad Ali, His Life and Times, p.326)

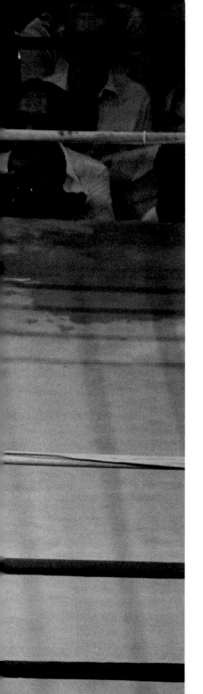

"Man, I hit him with punches that would
have brought down the walls of a city.
Lawdy, Lawdy, he's a great champion."

JOE FRAZIER post fight. (*Sports Illustrated*, 10.13.1975)

JOE FRAZIER GIVES BEGRUDGING RESPECT TO ALI
AFTER HIS 14TH-ROUND SURRENDER.

COOPMAN '76

CLEMENTE COLISEUM, HATO REY, PUERTO RICO. KO5. (RETAINED WORLD HEAVYWEIGHT TITLE)

"He's a gentleman. He smiled at me every day before the fight.

I'm glad he's not hurt."

MUHAMMAD ALI on Coopman. (*Associated Press*, 2.20.1976)

ALI WRAPS HIS OWN HANDS BEFORE HIS FIVE-ROUND CAKEWALK OVER BELGIUM'S JEAN-PIERRE COOPMAN, THE SO-CALLED "LION OF FLANDERS".

"I felt like 500 pounds were falling on me and I fell down. He was hard to hit.

He's a scientific fighter."

JEAN-PIERRE COOPMAN, (*Associated Press*, 2.20.1976)

YOUNG '76
vs. Jimmy Young
April 30, 1976

CAPITAL CENTER, LANDOVER, MARYLAND. W15. (RETAINED WORLD HEAVYWEIGHT TITLE)

"It was horrible. It was a nightmare. But I'll tell you this about Young. He didn't come after the title. He was the guy hanging his head through the ropes. When you're the challenger, you have to go out and win it. And he didn't do it … But I don't think Ali will take anyone so cheaply again. Frankly, *I wish there were five more Joe Fraziers or George Foremans for him to fight,* then I'd never have to worry about him keeping his mind on business."

ANGELO DUNDEE, (*Baltimore Sun*, 5.2.1976)

MANY RINGSIDE CRITICS, INCLUDING SPORTSCASTER HOWARD COSELL, WONDERED WHETHER ALI DESERVED HIS 15-ROUND DECISION OVER CRAFTY JIMMY YOUNG IN MARYLAND. YOUNG PROTESTED IN VAIN.

ENGLAND'S RICHARD DUNN SQUARES OFF WITH ALI, WHO USED HIM AS A PUNCHING BAG IN THEIR MUNICH BOUT.

DUNN '76

vs. Richard Dunn
May 24, 1976

OLYMPIAHALLE, MUNICH, GERMANY. KO5. (RETAINED WORLD HEAVYWEIGHT TITLE)

"Dunn was much better than I thought he was, but at the pace it was going, I knew he'd fade out after ten or 11 rounds. He was right in one way, making me work and do my best. I did the 'rope-a-dope' a couple of times and it came in handy. It saved me some work. **He gave me more trouble than I expected. He hit me real good a couple of times. I give him credit for a great match.**"

MUHAMMAD ALI. Richard Dunn was floored five times before referee Herbert Thomaser stopped it. (*Associated Press*, 5.25.1976)

NORTON '76

vs. Ken Norton
September 28, 1976

YANKEE STADIUM, NEW YORK CITY. W15. (RETAINED WORLD HEAVYWEIGHT TITLE)

"I was robbed. I won ten rounds, at least nine. The judges gave Ali the decision because they see him making a lot of money for boxing." KEN NORTON, (*Baltimore Sun*, 9.29.1976)

IT WAS ONE OF ALI'S BETTER MOMENTS IN HIS THIRD AND FINAL CLASH WITH KEN NORTON AT YANKEE STADIUM—ONE OF ALI'S MOST CONTROVERSIAL VICTORIES.

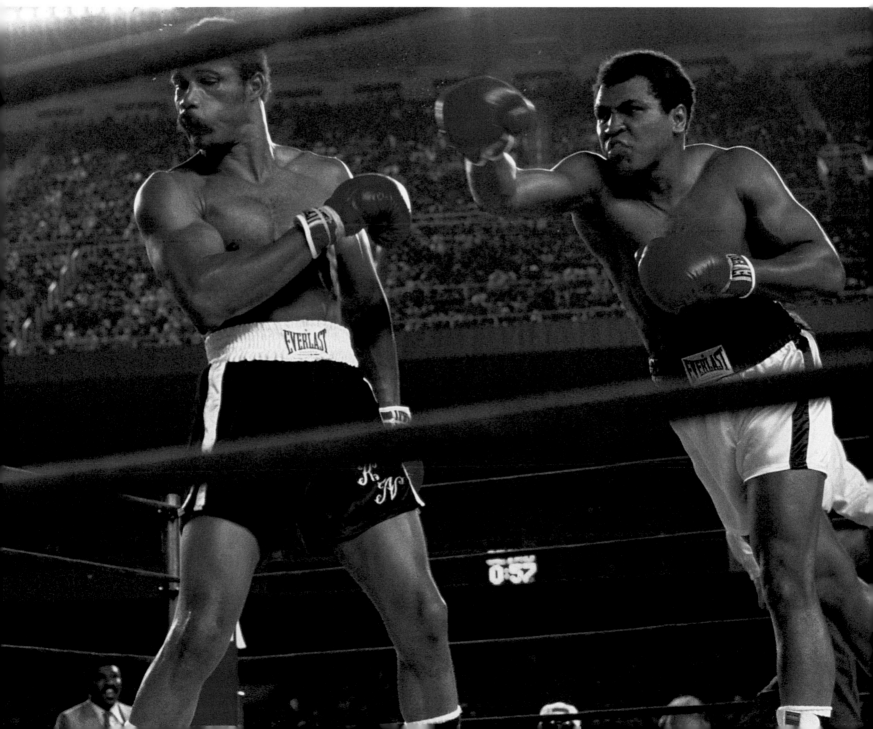

SEVEN
Spinks and Retirement

The *Rocky*-like scenario of Muhammad Ali's championship defense against Leon Spinks in Las Vegas on February 15, 1978, was too obvious and too appealing for the media to ignore. Leon Spinks, 24, a scruffy, uneducated, street brawler who spoke in an almost incomprehensible ghetto language and with a resume of only seven professional fights, seemed perfectly cast as "Rocky Balboa", the classic underdog.

Ali, a proud champion, had vanquished seemingly invincible foes in Sonny Liston and George Foreman and also whipped former heavyweight kings Floyd Patterson and Joe Frazier. Now, an aging 36 and showing visible signs of wear and tear, he seemed well suited for the role of "Apollo Creed".

Ali had the brash talk and swagger, but it took the guileless Spinks to put their upcoming fight in perspective. "That was a movie, this is reality." [1] he said after the contracts were signed, guaranteeing Ali $3.5 million compared to $320,000 for the lightly regarded challenger.

In fact, the first time Spinks' voluble manager, Butch Lewis, who was then working for promoter Bob Arum, proposed the match to Ali, he was greeted by derision. As Lewis recalled, "After Ali fought Earnie Shavers, he started talking like maybe he'd retire. I told him, 'Fine, but if you fight again, I'd like you to give Leon a shot.'

"Ali thought I was nuts. At the time, Leon had fought only five times as a pro. He told me, 'I can't fight this kid; it would make me the laughing stock of the world.' So I got Leon a fight with Scott LeDoux, a middle-of-the-road heavyweight. They put it on television because Leon was an Olympic gold medal winner. They fought to a draw, and I got a call from Ali, 'Butch, I want your boy bad,' he told me. He shouted, 'I beat Patterson, Foreman and Frazier, who all won gold medals. I'm gonna beat 'em all before I retire and prove I'm the greatest of all time.'" [2]

The championship fight still proved a tough sell. Of the major networks, only CBS showed interest. And the promotion suffered another setback when Ali surprisingly took a 'vow of silence', believing it was impossible to diminish Spinks any further in the public's eye.

Ali was a bloated 242 pounds when he began training and limited his sparring to less than 25 rounds. He sold Spinks short like the fight mob and Las Vegas gamblers who permitted wagers only on the 5–1 underdog.

No one fully understood the passion and hunger of the ex-Marine who first gained notoriety by winning the 175-pound gold medal in the 1976 Olympic Games. Foreman, who witnessed the event in Montreal, said, "Spinks is not a boxer, but he's the best street fighter I've seen." [3]

Compared to Spinks, Ali's youth was almost idyllic. Spinks needed to fight almost every day to survive the squalid streets of his hometown of St. Louis. The Pruitt-Igoe project where he lived for most of his adolescence was so infested by drugs and crime, the city decided the only solution was to demolish it.

"Our mother used to keep us in the house because we were always getting beat up," Spinks remembered. "They called me and my brother, Michael, 'messovers' because we were so easy to mess up." [4]

Inevitably, the Spinks brothers learned to fight back and won more than their share of street brawls. But the crime and senseless killings were too much to overcome.

"One day when I was 15," he said, "I walked out of our building and heard that a friend of mine had been killed. Then I heard another had been locked up. I looked around, looked at where I lived, and knew I had to do something with my life. I knew if I didn't get out of the neighborhood, I'd wind up dead or in jail, just like my friends. My dad used to beat me and say I'd never amount to nothing, calling me a fool out of the blue. I wanted the name of Spinks to mean something besides dirt. I wanted to be a somebody." [5]

So, it was understandable that Spinks failed to hold Ali in awe, even if he had served as his ring idol.

A year before their fight, Spinks recalls sharing a ride with Ali from the Philadelphia airport. "On the way I was kidding him," Spinks said. "I told him that I had broken into his house, tried on his championship belt, and it was a perfect fit. And that I'd also tried on his crown, but that was just a little big." [6]

But there were more concrete reasons for Spinks' air of confidence. Like a national audience, he had witnessed Ali's life-and-death struggle with Shavers five months earlier in New York when the badly battered champion escaped with a questionable 15-round decision.

Some of Ali's staunchest allies were not fooled. "Muhammad is 36 years-old. He's at the end of the rainbow," [7] said long-time trainer, Angelo Dundee.

Ferdie Pacheco, his personal physician, was even more candid.

Said Pacheco, "If I had to pick a spot to tell him, 'You've got all your marbles, don't go on anymore,' it would have been after he beat Frazier in Manila. He began to take beatings, not just in fights, but in the ring.

"The Shavers fight was the final straw for me. After that fight Dr. Vincent Nardiello, the New York Commission doctor, gave me a lab report showing Ali's kidneys were falling apart. I wrote a letter about his physical condition and sent copies to Ali's manager, Herbert Muhammad, his wife, Veronica, and to Dundee. No one answered. That's when I decided enough was enough. They were talking about putting Ali 'only in easy fights', but there was no such thing as an easy fight anymore." [8]

Pacheco's concerns were vindicated by Ali's inept performance against such an inexperienced foe. When Ali entered the ring, a respectful Spinks joined in the applause. But the cheering soon ended.

Spinks refused to be conned by Ali's ring legerdemain or taunting during the bout. Amazingly, he had answers and counters for the champion's endless bag of tricks. He effectively cut off the ring, employed a relentless body attack when Ali resorted to his patented "Rope-a-Dope" tactics, and, in the so-called "championship" rounds, used his youth and superior conditioning to survive a desperate comeback by a fading champion.

The fact that his crown was slipping away was not lost on Ali, who confided to Dundee after the eighth round, "He's young, soooo young." [9]

Life imitated art. "Rocky" had won again. Ali was gracious at the post-fight press conference. "I messed up. I was lousy," he said. "But I don't want to take anything away from Spinks. He fought a good fight and never quit. He made a fool of everybody, even me." [10]

Hours later, after listening to his sycophants assure him he was still the champion, Ali, his handsome face now badly bruised, headed for the hotel elevator to join the crowd in the casino below. Security guards formed a phalanx around him, but Ali broke loose and said, "You guys don't have to protect me. Nobody wants to touch me." [11]

In retrospect, it would be Ali's most embarrassing loss, knowing he had cheated himself in training and abandoned his title to a young fighter with limited skills. He could not bear to end his legendary career on such a bitter note. But the evidence was irrefutable. The aging lion was losing both his bite and roar. Like the fabled picture of Dorian Gray, he had suddenly grown old and vulnerable before the eyes of the world.

EVANGELISTA '77
vs. Alfredo Evangelista
May 16, 1977

CAPITAL CENTER, LANDOVER, MARYLAND. W15. (RETAINED WORLD HEAVYWEIGHT TITLE)

ALI'S FADING SKILLS WERE AGAIN CLEARLY IN EVIDENCE IN HIS LACKLUSTER VICTORY OVER TRIALHORSE ALFREDO EVANGELISTA.

"I kept asking Ali, **'Why don't you stop running, stand still and fight?'** But I said it in Spanish, and, I guess, Ali didn't understand me."

ALFREDO EVANGELISTA, (*Baltimore Sun*, 5.17.1977)

"In my Sonny Liston days, when I was young, **I would have eaten Evangelista up**. But not today. I can't do it anymore. Once I found out he could take a punch, I had to dance."

MUHAMMAD ALI, (*Baltimore Sun*, 5.17.1977)

"He was once an immortal.

Now he has come down from the mountain top to mortality and people are still expecting miracles."

Promoter **DON KING** on Muhammad Ali's lackluster performance. (*Baltimore Sun*, 5.17.1977)

(ABOVE) ALI RESORTS TO "ROPE-A-DOPE" TACTICS AGAINST A CHARGING EVANGELISTA AND FACES THE PRESS (BELOW).

SHAVERS '77

vs. Earnie Shavers
September 29, 1977

MADISON SQUARE GARDEN, NEW YORK CITY. W15. (RETAINED WORLD HEAVYWEIGHT TITLE)

"New York wants big championship fights, **but they don't deserve one the way they judge fights.** They stole one here from Ken Norton against Ali, and now another one tonight."

Shavers' trainer, FRANK LUCA, (*Baltimore Sun*, 9.30.1977)

GRABBING EARNIE SHAVERS' BALD PATE, ALI MOCKS ANGER FOR
THE CROWD AT MADISON SQUARE GARDEN.

"My corner told me I was ahead and that I won it. Ali's a bad champion. He didn't win it. **He was standing around posing, not fighting.**"

EARNIE SHAVERS, (*Baltimore Sun*, 9.30.1977)

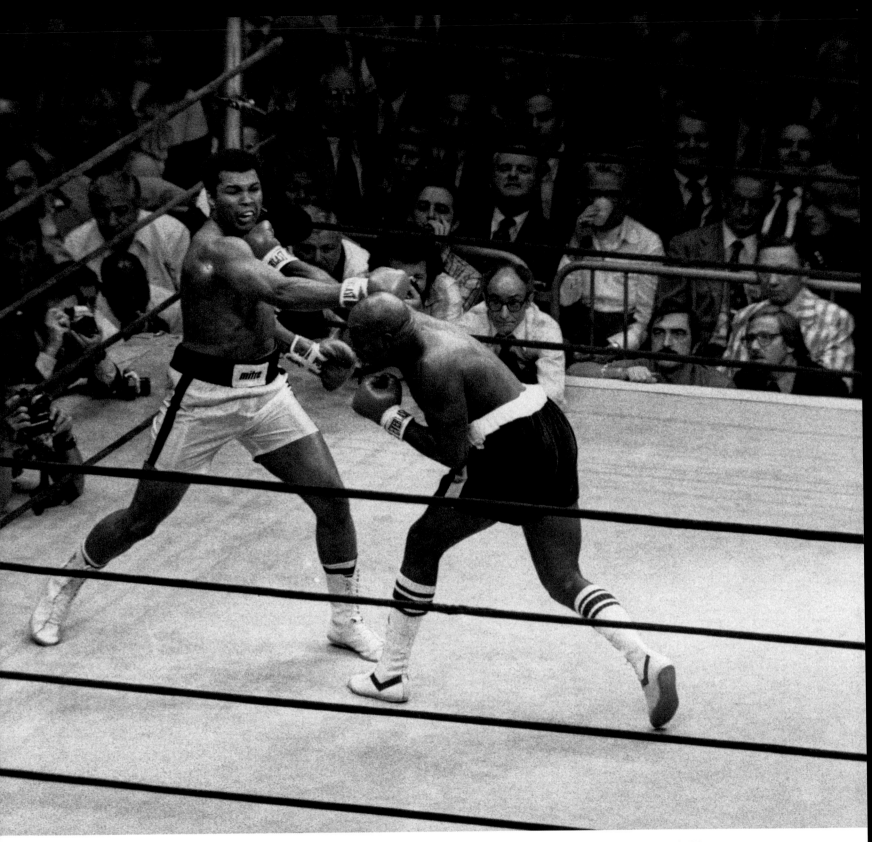

SEVERAL OF ALI'S CONFIDANTS URGED HIM TO RETIRE AFTER ABSORBING SUCH PHYSICAL PUNISHMENT IN A BRUTAL BATTLE WITH SHAVERS.

"I haven't been this tired since I fought Joe Frazier in Manila. You've got to realize I've got a lot of heart. I'm a real champion. **My hands hurt, my knees hurt, my back hurts. I'm 35 years old. With the wear and tear I've been through, it's a miracle I did this for 15 rounds."**

MUHAMMAD ALI, (*Baltimore Sun,* 9.30.1977)

SPINKS '78

vs. Leon Spinks
February 15, 1978

LAS VEGAS HILTON, LAS VEGAS, NEVADA. L15. (LOST WORLD HEAVYWEIGHT TITLE)

"That was a movie, this is reality."

LEON SPINKS, pre-fight, on his being compared to filmdom's classic underdog, "Rocky".

(*Philadelphia Inquirer*, 2.10.1978)

"Of all the fights I lost, losing to Spinks hurt the most.

That's because it was my fault. Leon did the best he could, but it was embarrassing someone with so little fighting skills could beat me. I didn't train right. I gave away the first six rounds, figuring he'd tire out, and it turned out I got tired. I just couldn't leave boxing that way. It was too embarrassing."

MUHAMMAD ALI in retrospect. (Thomas Hauser, *Muhammad Ali, His Life and Times*, p.353)

"I got guts. I got a big heart. I will fight any man with two arms, two feet and one head. My biggest credential is my birth certificate. I got 12 years on Ali.

Let's face it. He's an old man."

LEON SPINKS, (*Philadelphia Inquirer,* 2.9.1978)

"We all lose in life. You lose your wife, you lose your mother. We all have losses, **and what you have to do is keep living, overcome those losses and come back.** You can't just go and die because you lose."

MUHAMMAD ALI on his defeat.

(*Sports Illustrated,* 2.17.1978)

LEON SPINKS DISPLAYED SURPRISING BOXING
SKILLS AND RESOURCEFULNESS IN UPSETTING
AN ILL-PREPARED ALI IN LAS VEGAS.

DESPITE HAVING HAD ONLY SEVEN PROFESSIONAL FIGHTS, LEON SPINKS STILL FOUND A WAY TO VANQUISH ALI.

"You're sitting at ringside drinking beer and you think you're surprised? **I was in the ring getting my ass whipped. You know I was surprised."**

MUHAMMAD ALI talking to the media after the fight. (John Schulian, *Writers' Fighters*, p.16)

"I messed up. I was lousy. But I don't want to take anything away from Spinks. He fought a good fight and never quit. **He made a fool out of everybody, even me."**

MUHAMMAD ALI post fight (*New York Post*, 2.16.1978)

GAP-TOOTHED LEON SPINKS EXALTS IN TRIUMPH AFTER DETHRONING ALI IN A STUNNING UPSET.

SPINKS '78

vs. Leon Spinks
September 15, 1978

SUPERDROME, NEW ORLEANS, LOUISIANA. W15. (REGAINED WORLD HEAVYWEIGHT TITLE)

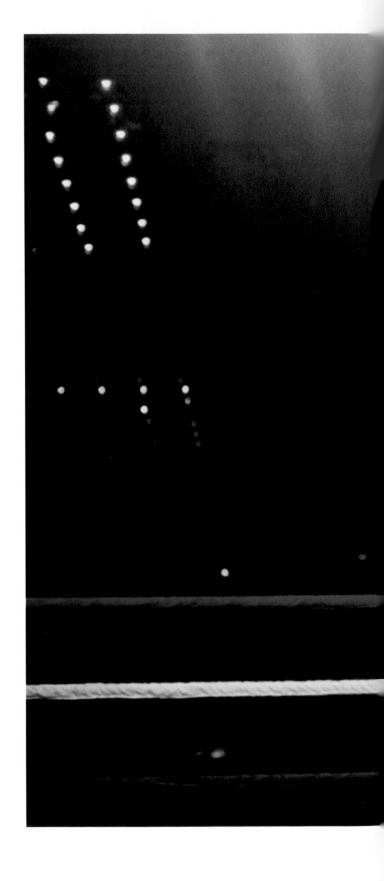

"This will be my 'Third Coming'.

My first coming was in 1964
when I shocked the world
by beating Sonny Liston.
My second coming was
when I upset George Foreman
in Zaire in 1974.
My third coming will be
against Spinks tonight."

Pre-fight **MUHAMMAD ALI,** (*Baltimore Sun*, 9.15.1978)

ALI TORTURED HIS BODY IN PREPARATION FOR HIS REMATCH WITH
LEON SPINKS IN NEW ORLEANS, WHILE SPINKS ACTED AS PLAYBOY.

"A lot of people never saw Einstein, FDR or Jesus, for that matter. **Everybody dies, and everybody grows old. I've been around since 1961.** I've lasted longer than the Beatles and the Supremes. Now it's just me and the Rolling Stones."

More pre-fight **MUHAMMAD ALI,** (*Baltimore Sun,* 9.12.1978)

ALI TAKES COVER AS SPINKS, SENSING HIS CROWN SLIPPING, GETS SET TO LAUCH A RIGHT.

"Did you ever see a 36-year-old man outlast a 25-year-old man like that?"

MUHAMMAD ALI post fight. (*Baltimore Sun*, 9.16.1978)

"I'm ready this time.

It would have been a disaster if I hadn't got another shot

at the title, and I realize this is my last chance.

I'll show Spinks to be the amateur he really is.

As bad as I was the last time,

I was still even going into the 13th.

Doesn't that tell you something."

MUHAMMAD ALI, (*Baltimore Sun*, 9.15.1978)

BUNDINI BROWN (RIGHT) GIVES ENCOURAGEMENT TO ALI ON HIS WAY TO REGAINING THE CROWN.

The Comeback

Muhammad Ali, who enjoyed performing magic tricks, often boasted, "I'm a master of illusion. I make you see something that you really don't see." [1] But pulling a silver coin out of an unsuspecting kid's ear or making two pieces of rope whole again would prove a lot easier for the three-time heavyweight champion than convincing the world that, at 38, and coming off a two-year retirement following an inspiring victory over Leon Spinks to regain his title, he was still capable of beating Larry Holmes, the reigning champion, who was just reaching the prime of his boxing life.

As Ali's legion of worshipers would sadly learn in Las Vegas the night of October 2, 1980, this was one trick he was incapable of pulling off. Pride goeth before the fall. He had tried to "sucker punch" Holmes and the fight crowd by dying his graying hair black and by undergoing a tortuous seven-month crash diet that transformed his flabby 254-pound frame into a deceptively svelte 217.

The gamblers bought into the scam. The opening odds of 3–1 favoring Holmes shrunk to 13–10 by fight night. They believed the human butterfly, who had brought so much color and excitement to the ring for close to two decades was ready to spread his wings again.

The day before the fight, Ali displayed his boyish figure to the press gallery and bellowed, "This is the first miracle. You will witness an even bigger miracle when I knock Holmes out." [2]

Performing miracles had become almost as commonplace for Ali as the late Harry Houdini. For years he had mesmerized fans and judges with his sleight of hand. Even at an advanced age, he managed to gain questionable decisions over Ken Norton and Jimmy Young by convincing his audience he could still dance for 15 rounds.

But Ali was only fooling himself. Seeing is not always believing. Four months before he challenged Holmes, boxing writers recalled Ali holding an impromptu press conference in Montreal prior to the welterweight showdown between Roberto Duran and Sugar Ray Leonard. He stumbled on his way to the podium and carefully buttoned his waistcoat to hide his bulging beltline. He resembled an overstuffed zombie as he delivered a lengthy monologue, often slurring his words.

His "Fourth Coming" would prove a cruel hoax. As his long-time physician, Ferdie Pacheco, noted prior to the fight, "When old talents fail, and all that is left is guile, experience, cunning and will—I know Ali has stepped into his past. His body is dead." [3]

Pacheco was not the only one concerned with Ali's well-being. Before granting him a license, the Nevada State Athletic Commission ordered Ali to undergo an extensive two-day neurological examination at the famed Mayo Clinic in Minnesota. The doctors' report revealed that Ali experienced "occasional tingling" in his hands in the morning and that the aging fighter was aware of slurring his speech for the past 10 or 12 years.

Still, the doctors found no reason for Nevada to refuse Ali a license on physical grounds. And there was always someone in Ali's camp to massage his ego and assure him he was still capable of defying the laws of nature.

"Sure," said veteran trainer Angelo Dundee, "his reflexes aren't what they were ten years, or even two years ago. But he has learned to compensate for that with his experience and ring generalship. He can make just about anyone fight his fight. We're talking about Ali who is truly unique. Compared to Ali, the rest of them are mere earthlings." [4]

Unfortunately, for Ali, the one man who wouldn't buy into the hype was Holmes, who knew Ali all too well, having served as his sparring partner when he was preparing for the

"Rumble in the Jungle" with George Foreman and "The Thrilla in Manila" with Joe Frazier.

"I respected and worshiped him," said Holmes. "He would introduce me to the press as 'the future heavyweight champ'. He taught me all the fundamentals and how to behave and carry yourself like a champion. I'd sit in his dressing room and listen to him talk like God was preaching to me." [5]

But from the day the fight was signed, with Ali guaranteed $8 million and Holmes, the champion, agreeing to $5 million, he realized it was a "no-win" situation. If he spoiled Ali's bid to become heavyweight champion a record fourth time, he knew that the public would either dismiss him as a shabby caretaker of the heavyweight title until Ali reclaimed his rightful place on the throne or that he would be remembered for reducing a legend to a 38-year-old "has-been" ravaged by age and too many blood-letting battles.

"I can't worry about this anymore," he said. "I can't be concerned if people say I beat up an old man. It's time to get the monkey off my back. I'm going to hurt Ali. This is something I never wanted to do. He's got to be down on his knees before I look to the referee to help him. I'm fighting for Larry Holmes' identity." [6]

But as the sorry spectacle unfolded, Holmes could only feel compassion for his fading idol who was serving as a punching bag. By the fourth round, he was wearing an expression that indicated he preferred being anywhere but in the same ring with Ali. He asked long-time trainer Richie Giachetti, "What am I supposed to do? You want me to keep beating on him? Don't everybody realize I can hit him at will?" [7]

In the opposite corner, Dundee, blanching at the carnage, was beseeching Ali to fight or quit. Minus his hand speed, punch and legs, Ali was clearly a man who had run out of miracles. By the middle rounds, the atmosphere in the makeshift arena built on the parking lot of Caesars Palace had taken on a funereal air with the stunned crowd of 24,740 acting like mourners attending a wake for a fallen hero. As Sylvester Stallone, the creator of the *Rocky* fable, observed from ringside, "It was like watching an autopsy on a man who's still alive." [8]

In the ninth round, Holmes landed a vicious uppercut to the ribs that sent Ali flying against the ropes. Recalled Holmes, "I hit him the hardest shots I ever threw. He'd begin to fall, and then it was like something clicked and wouldn't let him. He'd straighten up, and I said, 'Why are you takin' this?' And he said, 'C'mon, and fight sucker.'" [9]

Mercifully, the horrific beating ended after the tenth round when Dundee informed referee Richard Greene that Ali was finished. His shaman, Bundini Brown urged Dundee to allow Ali one more round. But Dundee broke loose and yelled, "Screw you! I'm the chief second. The ball game's over." [10]

Hours later, they drifted into Ali's hotel suite to pay their last respects—old friends, relatives, sycophants and hangers-on coming to view the battered body that had sounded like a death rattle in the ring. A tearful Holmes led the procession, urging Ali to give up the ghost.

"I respect you and love you," said Holmes. "I didn't want to hurt you out there." [11]

But Ali refused to accept the idea that he had turned old overnight. "I don't think it was a matter of age," he said. "I think I became dehydrated by dieting and training too hard. I had no strength. After round one, I told myself, 'I'm so tired. I'm in trouble.' My idea was to go out fighting, but I just couldn't do it." [12]

Later, it would be revealed that Ali had been misdiagnosed for a hypothyroid condition and had been popping the drug Thyrolar like vitamin pills, thinking it would serve as a stimulant. In fact, the results were just the opposite, making him lethargic and short of breath, hardly the prescription for engaging in a major fight. The physician, Dr. Charles Williams, acknowledged, "I may have placed him in jeopardy inadvertently." [13]

But the bad medical advise was only part of Ali's growing problem. The master illusionist had simply lost his ability to perform his magic act inside the ropes. He was no longer Superman, but all too human. The "long goodbye" had begun.

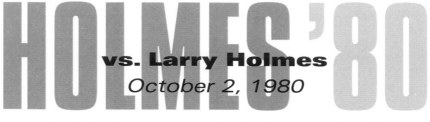

HOLMES '80
vs. Larry Holmes
October 2, 1980

CAESER'S PALACE, LAS VEGAS, NEVADA. LKO BY 11. (FOR WORLD HEAVYWEIGHT TITLE)

"I got it made for life financially, and every other way. I don't have to beat Larry Holmes. Why? I raised him. He was my sparring partner for three years."

MUHAMMAD ALI before Holmes fight.

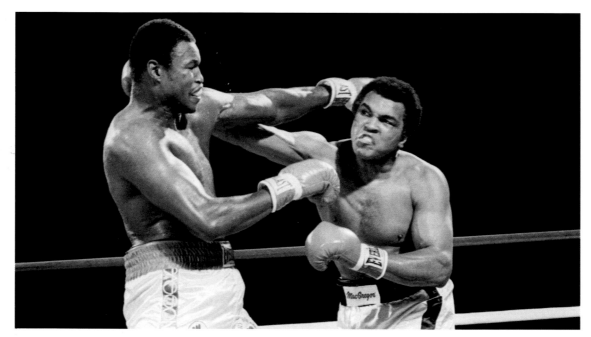

(ABOVE) LARRY HOLMES ALMOST SEEMS TO BE PLAYING WITH HIS FORMER MENTOR AND REPEATEDLY
ASKED THE REFEREE TO SAVE ALI FROM FURTHER PUNISHMENT. (RIGHT) ALI BECKONS ACROSS THE RING,
BUT ANGELO DUNDEE IS PREPARED TO END HIS BEATING BY LARRY HOLMES.

"After the fight, I went to Ali's hotel room and told him, *'You're the greatest, I love you.'*

I meant it, and I felt awful. Even though I won, I was down. And Muhammad said to me,
'Man, I'm mad. I took care of you, fed you and taught you how to fight. And look what you
did to me.' I want people to know I'm proud I learned my craft from Ali.
I'm prouder of sparring with him when he was young than of beating him when he was old."

LARRY HOLMES, (Thomas Hauser, *Muhammad Ali, His Life and Times,* p.413)

BERBICK '81

vs. Trevor Berbick
December 11, 1981

QEII SPORTS CENTRE, NASSAU, BAHAMAS. L10.

"People tell me not to fight, but they are at the foot of the wall of knowledge and I'm at the top.

My horizon is greater than theirs. Why do people go to the moon? Why did Martin Luther King

say he had a dream? **People need challenges.**

What's wrong with me trying to win the title a fourth time?

You ever see so many people worry about one black guy in your life?"

MUHAMMAD ALI, (*New York Times*, 11.19.1981)

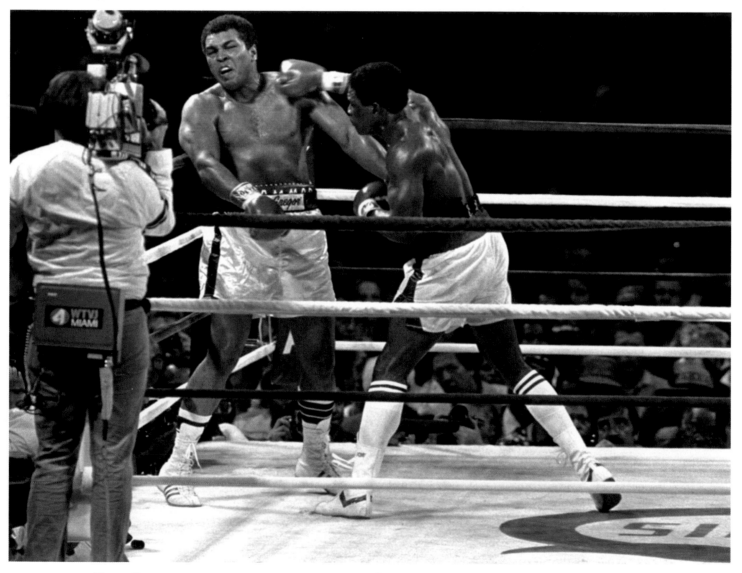

TREVOR BERBICK WAS IN TOTAL CONTROL OF THIS FIGHT IN THE BAHAMAS THAT PROVED SUCH A PAINFUL FAREWELL FOR ALI.

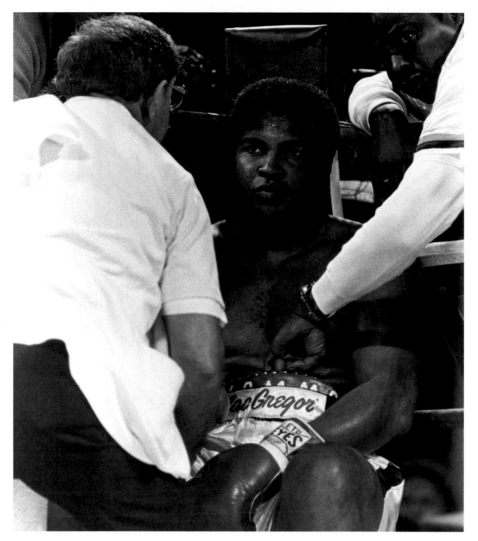

LONGTIME TRAINER, ANGELO DUNDEE, ALREADY KNOWS THAT
ALI HAS NO MORE TO GIVE IN HIS SWANSONG VERSUS BERBICK.

Six months later, Ali contemplated a comeback and discussed the idea with Dundee.

Ali: "What do you think about me fighting again?"

Dundee: "You can't do it anymore. *There isn't any water left in the well.*"

JOHN SCHULIAN, *Writers' Fighters*, p.38

EIGHT

The Legend Lives On

"He is fascinating; *attraction and repulsion in the same package.*

He is America's greatest Ego.

But he is also the very spirit of the 20th Century,

the prince of mass man and the media."

NORMAN MAILER on Muhammad Ali.

I t was an early December night in New York, and Muhammad Ali was called to the stage at Madison Square Garden to receive a trophy presented by *Sports Illustrated* signifying him as the "Sportsman of the Century". For the huge gathering in the arena, including such sports legends as Pele, Michael Jordan, Jack Nicklaus, Magic Johnson and Carl Lewis, it was a painful sight.

The three-time heavyweight champion who dominated the boxing scene for close to two decades with his unique ring talents and magnetic personality, no longer floated like a butterfly. The feet that once gave us the patented "Ali Shuffle" now moved through life in slow motion, each step an obvious chore. And his once-lightning hands now shook almost uncontrollably, the result of his 57-year-old body ravaged by Parkinson's syndrome, a neurological disorder that also slurs his speech.

But soon the big arena was filled with the chant "Ali, Ali, Ali" in tribute to the man who transcended his sport. It was the same encouraging sounds he heard in this building in the mid-70s when he staged two of his memorable brawls with arch-rival Joe Frazier.

Ali could always orchestrate major events, everything but the ending of his ring career. In the winter of 1981, in Nassau of all places, he made his sorrowful exit, losing a ten-round decision to journeyman Trevor Berbick. It was a fight no one wanted, save Ali, who had preferred going out a winner after his humbling beating by then heavyweight champion, Larry Holmes, a former sparring partner.

But this time he promised there would be no more encores. "Father Time caught up with me," he said. "I'm finished. For the first time I feel that I'm 40 years old. I know it's the end. I'm not crazy. We all lose sometimes. We all grow old." [1]

Still, no one was prepared for the medical report in 1984 that he was suffering from Parkinson's syndrome. His ability to take a punch in his 61-bout career had not served him well, particularly when he resorted to his "Rope-A-Dope" tactics and absorbed unusual punishment at the hands of George Foreman, Joe Frazier and Larry Holmes.

For a brief time, Ali contemplated undergoing a medical procedure performed by a Mexican surgeon who would implant adrenal gland tissue in the brain. But the experiment had a ten percent mortality rate. Ali walked to the edge, then backed off and accepted his fate.

"I know why this happened," he said. "I'm just a man like everyone else. People think I'm suffering, but I ain't suffering. I was suffering when they wouldn't let me box during the Vietnam War. What if I had finished undefeated? What if I'd won my last two fights? If I didn't have this health problem, I'd be talking like I used to, trying to keep up with my image, doing all those interviews and commercials. It wouldn't be human." [2]

Relying on his strong spirituality to overcome any feelings of melancholy, Ali, with his fourth wife, Lonnie, now spends most of his days in serenity on his 88-acre farm in Berrien Springs, Michigan, in the heartland of America. Most of his time is devoted to prayers, reading the *Koran* and propagating his Islamic faith by signing hundreds of religious tracts for worldwide distribution.

It is a far cry from his tumultuous times in the 1960s and '70s, when he might have been the world's most-recognizable face, known to more people than Elvis Presley or the Pope, but always an enigma. For Ali was always bigger than life, part fact, part myth. His fame was so overwhelming that during his historic visit to the Philippines in 1975 for his "Thrilla In Manila" with Frazier, the nation's president, Ferdinand Marcos, said in half-jest, "If you were a Filipino, I'd have you shot." [3]

Said Ali, "I didn't realize how bold I was until I look back on those days. I came along at a time when the whole nation was changing. Malcolm X got shot for his preaching. Martin Luther King was fighting for integration, and I was sitting on a dais with Elijah Muhammad, who was saying all white men are devils. I was either bold or crazy." [4]

He was always more than a super-jock, breaking past the limited boundaries of sports and confidently mingling with presidents, kings and world leaders on every continent. In 1980, President Jimmy Carter used Ali as his emissary to Africa to explain why the United States was boycotting the 1980 Olympic Games in Moscow.

No longer restricted by the confines of a boxing ring, Ali now made the world his stage and the media masses followed in his wake. "I'm not bragging," he said after hanging up his gloves, "but I'm more loved than all the superstars in the world combined. I was blessed to come along when I did. If I had to pay for my press, it would have cost me $100 billion. You won't see another like me for 200 years." [5]

For all the divisiveness he had caused with his braggadocio style, his transformation to the Muslim faith and his anti-war stand, Ali was now universally loved. In recent years, Ali, accompanied by his wife and biographer, Thomas Hauser, has toured schools across the United States to talk about racial healing. And an $80 million downtown riverfront center is being built in his hometown of Louisville to celebrate his career as a boxer, but, more importantly, as a way to reach the youth with messages of tolerance for their ethnic neighbors.

"Just don't call it a museum," said Lonnie Ali, who, when she was 17 and living across the street from then Cassius Clay, determined she would one day become his wife. "This is about what he stood for, what he paid a price for. I want it done while he's alive so the kids who come can actually touch him." [6]

Sports sociologist, Richard Lapchick, drew an interesting analogy between Ali and O.J. Simpson, another American superstar whose football career spanned the same era. Wrote Lapchick: "Both had incredible athletic careers. Both became beloved by the public and crossed racial lines. O.J. seemed to spend his life trying to prove there was no divide between the races. Ali's legacy included standing up as a proud black man and emphasizing boldly that race does matter. To this day, no other athlete has done that so effectively.

"It seems ironic that one accused of dividing the races now roams free but lives in disgrace in the eyes of the majority of Americans. The other, who was accused of dividing the races because he stood tall as a black American, now brings people of all racial groups together by preaching 'healing'." [7]

With each passing year, Ali has grown in stature. On a summer night in Atlanta in 1996, some three billion people around the world watched the poignant spectacle of Ali, forgetting all his infirmities, carrying the Olympic torch and walking up to the top of the stadium to light the flame that would begin the Olympic Games.

"Muhammad wouldn't go to bed for hours that night," *Lonnie Ali recalled.*

"He was floating on air.

He just sat in his chair back at the hotel holding the torch in his hands.

It was like he'd won the heavyweight title a fourth time." [8]

ALI LIGHTS THE OLYMPIC TORCH FOR THE 1996 GAMES IN ATLANTA.

The whole world was touched as Ali, overcoming his infirmities, carries the Olympic torch.

And how does Ali choose to be remembered?

"I'd like to be remembered as a black man who won the heavyweight title, was humorous and treated everyone right. As a man who never looked down on those who looked up to him and who helped as many of his people as he could—financially and also in their fight for freedom, justice and equality. As a man who tried to unite his people through the faith of Islam. And if all that's asking too much, I'd settle for being remembered as a boxing champion who became a preacher and champion of his people." [9]

It was not too much to ask of a man who has been described over the past 40 years as a clown, a prophet, a hero, a villain, an agitator and a peacemaker. He was one and all of the above. More, much more. Truly, one of a kind. Simply, "The Greatest."

"Ali created a new relationship between the boxers,

the press and the spectators. He went beyond the borders of boxing.

His best fight was the one he lost to Joe Frazier.

He suffered that night,

but he was honest with himself and boxing.

When you lose, you show how big you are."

Former middleweight champion, **NINO BENVENUTI**.

ALI TRIES ON THE OLYMPIC MEDAL FOR SIZE, SURROUNDED BY MEMBERS OF AMERICA'S CHAMPIONSHIP BASKETBALL TEAM.

JOE FRAZIER AND GEORGE FOREMAN JOIN ALI IN ONCE AGAIN HEARING THE ROAR OF THE CROWD.

"I first met Muhammad Ali the night of our first fight in 1973.

At that time, Ali was boxing.
If you got to fight him, even if you lost,
it was good for your name,

You either liked Ali and wanted him to win or disliked him
and wanted him to get beat. But, regardless, you watched him."

KEN NORTON, former heavyweight champion.

"In a way, Muhammad Ali is like everybody's cousin. He was seen by everybody as one of their own. The heavyweight champion of the world beats people up, but when you were near him, you never felt fear. He could walk up to somebody's door at 3 a.m. and say, 'I have a flat tire.' And, if they looked out the door, they'd say, 'Hey, that's Muhammad Ali.' And they would come outside. Ali is that familiar, but in a remarkable way.

Mike Tyson is familiar,
but you wouldn't want him coming to your door at 3 a.m.'

KAREEM ABDUL-JABBAR, (*GQ*, April, 1998)

MIKE TYSON GETS WORDS OF ADVICE FROM ALI.

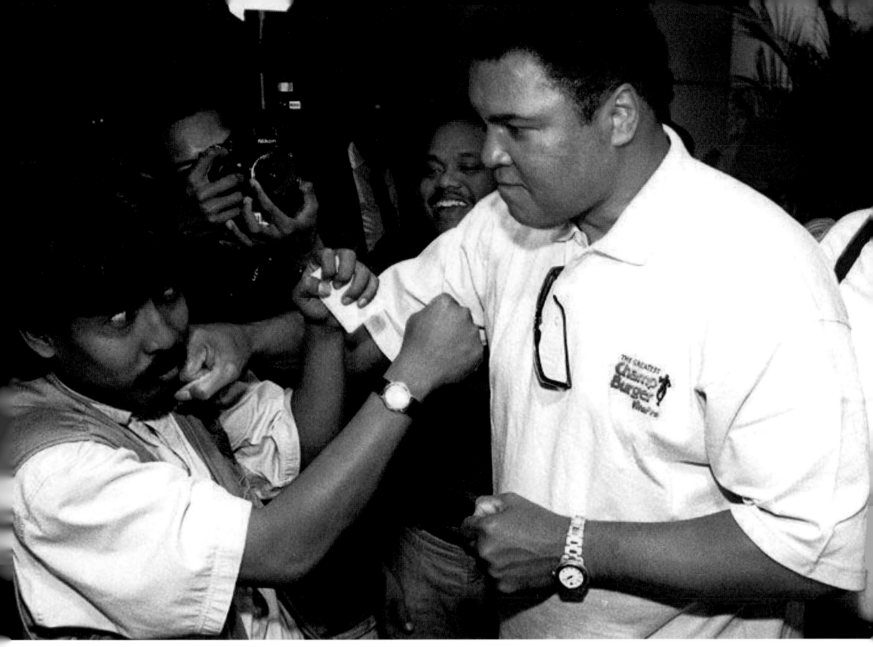

ALI SHOWS A WILLING ADMIRER HOW TO DELIVER A RIGHT TO THE CHIN DURING A VISIT TO INDONESIA.

"I've been offered deals to do boxing promotions, to speak and make business deals. I've turned them all down to promote world peace. Sheiks of Arabia will donate money, certain people will donate the airplane. It's going to be beautiful. Powerful. **Boxing was Allah's way of getting me fame to do something bigger.** *This is ten times bigger than boxing.*"

MUHAMMAD ALI, before embarking on UN-sponsored "Children's Journey For Peace". (*Washington Post*, 5.22.1983)

"JUST TRY ME," ALI SEEMS TO BE TELLING FANS DURING A UN-SPONSORED TRIP.

"Cassius had Caucasian images of God on his wall.
Ali was taught to believe there could be no image of God, no color.
That's a big difference. "

MUHAMMAD ALI, when asked to describe difference between Cassius Clay and Muhammad Ali. (*New York Times,* 4.28.1985)

(ABOVE) AFTER RETIRING FROM THE RING, A GLOBETROTTING ALI SPENT TIME IN AUSTRALIA. (RIGHT) WITH HIS PASSION FOR PERFORMING MAGIC TRICKS, ALI APPEARS TO BE THINKING OF HOW HE CAN STILL FOOL THE PUBLIC.

"I've seen the whole world. I learn somethin' from people everywhere. There's truth in Hinduism. Christianity, Islam, all religions. And in just plain talkin'.
The only religion that matters is the real religion—*love.*"

MUHAMMAD ALI, (*Detroit News,* 1.17.1997)

"He (God) gave me Parkinson's syndrome to show me I'm not 'The Greatest', he is. To show me I have human frailties like everybody else does. That's all I am; a man."

MUHAMMAD ALI during an interview in 1987.

(ABOVE) AS USUAL ALI WAS ACCORDED VIP TREATMENT IN MELBOURNE.
(LEFT) ASSISTED BY A MOUNTED POLICEMAN, ALI POINTS A FINGER
TOWARD A WELL-WISHER DURING A VISIT TO THE LONDON
BOROUGH OF BRIXTON.

"People think I'm sufferin'. People thought I was sufferin' when they wouldn't let me box during the Vietnam War. I want my health back but *I ain't sufferin'.*

If I didn't have this health problem, I'd be talkin' like I used to, trying to keep up with my image, still doing all those interviews, commercials and speeches. **I'd probably have a miserable life. I wouldn't be human."**

MUHAMMAD ALI, (*Sports Ilustrated*, 11.15.1989)

Like Father, Like Daughter

Grudge match, family feud or just what's in a name? Whatever the case, it almost seems inevitable that Ali-Frazier IV will happen. No, not another brawl between the storied heavyweight champions who staged a classic ring trilogy in the Seventies, but their daughters, Laila and Jacqui, who want to keep the tradition alive by settling things with their fists.

Laila, 21, and the youngest of Muhammad Ali's nine children, was the first to follow in her father's footsteps. Possessed with the same intense pride, she wanted to make her own way in the labyrinthine world of professional boxing.

"I would have love to have been a person who was not Muhamad Ali's daughter, and got my experience boxing without everyone watching," Laila told *Ebony* magazine. "People were in my face from the beginning of my career, when I didn't know anything yet, trying to judge me. It was just too soon."

Seeing Laila in the ring creates mixed emotions for Muhammad. "He's happy that I'm happy," she said. "But if I told him I was through boxing, he'd probably say 'Whew!'"

Jacqui Frazier-Lyde's pursuit of a boxing career was more surprising. One of Joe's 11 children, she is 38, an attorney and the mother of three children of her own. But she has the full support of her father who helped dub her "Sister Smoke".

Like her no-nonsense father, she gets right to the point. "If Laila Ali wants a piece of me, I'll kick her butt. That's what Fraziers do. We kick Ali butt. Just let me know when, where and how much money."

Those are fighting words. Get it on, and let the best woman win.

(RIGHT) LAILA ALI SAMPLES THE THRILL OF VICTORY AFTER MAKING HER SUCCESSFUL PRO DEBUT.
(BELOW) JOINED BY WIFE LONNIE AT RINGSIDE, ALI GIVES THE VICTORY SIGN.

Fight record

Date	Opponent	Result	Site
Oct 29, 1960	**Tunney Hunsaker**	W6	Freedom Hall, Louisville, Kentucky
Dec 27, 1960	**Herb Siler**	KO4	Auditorium, Miami Beach, Florida
Jan 17, 1961	**Tony Esperti**	KO3	Auditorium, Miami Beach, Florida
Feb 7, 1961	**Jim Robinson**	KO1	Convention Hall, Miami Beach, Florida
Feb 21, 1961	**Donnie Fleeman**	KO7	Auditorium, Miami Beach, Florida
April 19, 1961	**Lamar Clark**	KO2	Freedom Hall, Louisville, Kentucky
June 26, 1961	**Duke Sabedong**	W10	Convention Center, Las Vegas, Nevada
July 22, 1961	**Alonzo Johnson**	W10	Freedom Hall, Louisville, Kentucky
Oct 7, 1961	**Alex Miteff**	KO6	Freedom Hall, Louisville, Kentucky
Nov 29, 1961	**Willi Besmanoff**	KO7	Freedom Hall, Louisville, Kentucky
Feb 10, 1961	**Sonny Banks**	KO4	Madison Square Garden, New York City
Feb 28, 1962	**Don Warner**	KO4	Convention Hall, Miami Beach, Florida
April 23, 1962	**George Logan**	KO4	Memorial Sports Arena, Los Angeles
May 19, 1962	**Billy Daniels**	KO7	St Nicholas Arena, New York City
July 20, 1962	**Alejandro Lavorante**	KO5	Memorial Sports Arena, Los Angeles
Nov 15, 1962	**Archie Moore**	KO4	Memorial Sports Arena, Los Angeles
Jan 24, 1963	**Charlie Powell**	KO3	Civic Arena, Pittsburgh, Pennsylvania

March 13, 1963	**Doug Jones**	W10	Madison Square Garden, New York City
June 18, 1963	**Henry Cooper**	KO5	Wembley Stadium, London, England
Feb 25, 1964	**Sonny Liston**	KO7	Convention Hall, Miami Beach, Florida *(Won the World Heavyweight title)*
May 25, 1965	**Sonny Liston**	KO1	St Dominick's Arena, Lewiston, Maine *(Retained the World Heavyweight title)*
Nov 22, 1965	**Floyd Patterson**	KO12	Convention Center, Las Vegas, Nevada *(Retained the World Heavyweight title)*
March 29, 1966	**George Chuvalo**	W15	Maple Leaf Gardens, Toronto, Canada *(Retained the World Heavyweight title)*
May 21, 1966	**Henry Cooper**	KO6	Highbury Stadium, London, England *(Retained the World Heavyweight title)*
Aug 6, 1966	**Brian London**	KO3	Earls Court, London, England *(Retained the World Heavyweight title)*
Sept 10, 1966	**Karl Mildenberger**	KO12	Wald Stadium, Frankfurt, Germany *(Retained the World Heavyweight title)*
Nov 14, 1966	**Cleveland Williams**	KO3	Astrodome, Houston, Texas *(Retained the World Heavyweight title)*
Feb 6, 1967	**Ernie Terrell**	W15	Astrodome, Houston, Texas *(Retained the World Heavyweight title)*
March 22, 1967	**Zora Folley**	KO7	Madison Square Garden, New York City *(Retained the World Heavyweight title)*

April 28, 1967: **Suspended for refusing induction into the US Army**

Oct 26, 1970	**Jerry Quarry**	KO3	Municipal Auditorium, Atlanta, Georgia
Dec 7, 1970	**Oscar Bonavena**	KO15	Madison Square Garden, New York City
March 8, 1971	**Joe Frazier**	L15	Madison Square Garden, New York City *(For the World Heavyweight title)*

July 26, 1971	**Jimmy Ellis**	KO12	Astrodome, Houston, Texas
Nov 17, 1971	**Buster Mathis**	W12	Astrodome, Houston, Texas
Dec 26, 1971	**Jürgen Blin**	KO7	Hallenstadion Arena, Zürich, Switzerland
April 1, 1972	**Mac Foster**	W15	Martial Arts Hall, Tokyo, Japan
May 1, 1972	**George Chuvalo**	W12	Pacific Coliseum, Vancouver, Canada
June 27, 1972	**Jerry Quarry**	KO7	Convention Center, Las Vegas, Nevada
July 19, 1972	**Al "Blue" Lewis**	KO11	Croke Park, Dublin, Ireland
Sept 20, 1972	**Floyd Patterson**	KO8	Madison Square Garden, New York City
Nov 21, 1972	**Bob Foster**	KO8	High Sierra Theatre, Stateline, Nevada
Feb 14, 1972	**Joe Bugner**	W12	Convention Center, Las Vegas, Nevada
March 31, 1973	**Ken Norton**	L12	Sports Arena, San Diego, California
Sept 10, 1973	**Ken Norton**	W12	Forum, Inglewood, California
Oct 20, 1973	**Rudi Lubbers**	W12	Senyan Stadium, Jakarta, Indonesia
Jan 28, 1974	**Joe Frazier**	W12	Madison Square Garden, New York City
Oct 30, 1974	**George Foreman**	KO8	20th of May Stadium, Kinshasa, Zaire *(Regained the World Heavyweight title)*
March 24, 1975	**Chuck Wepner**	KO15	Coliseum, Cleveland, Ohio *(Retained the World Heavyweight title)*
May 16, 1975	**Ron Lyle**	KO11	Convention Center, Las Vegas, Nevada *(Retained the World Heavyweight title)*
June 30, 1975	**Joe Bugner**	W15	Merdeka Stadium, Kuala Lumpur, Malaysia *(Retained the World Heavyweight title)*
Sept 10, 1975	**Joe Frazier**	KO15	Araheta Coliseum, Quezon City, Philippines

Feb 20, 1976	**Jean-Pierre Coopman**	KO5	Clemente Coliseum, Hato Rey, Puerto Rico *(Retained the World Heavyweight title)*
April 30, 1976	**Jimmy Young**	W15	Capital Center, Landover, Maryland *(Retained the World Heavyweight title)*
May 24, 1976	**Richard Dunn**	KO5	Olymphiahalle, Munich, Germany *(Retained the World Heavyweight title)*
Sept 28, 1976	**Ken Norton**	W15	Yankee Stadium, New York City *(Retained the World Heavyweight title)*
May 16, 1977	**Alfredo Evangelista**	W15	Capital Center, Landover, Maryland *(Retained the World Heavyweight title)*
Sept 29, 1977	**Earnie Shavers**	W15	Madison Square Garden, New York City *(Retained the World Heavyweight title)*
Feb 15, 1978	**Leon Spinks**	L15	Las Vegas Hilton, Las Vegas, Nevada *(Lost the World Heavyweight title)*
Sept 15, 1978	**Leon Spinks**	W15	Superdrome, New Orleans, Louisiana *(Regained the World Heavyweight title)*
June 27, 1979:	**Announces his retirement**		
Oct 2, 1980	**Larry Holmes**	KO by 11	Caesers Palace, Las Vegas, Nevada *(For the World Heavyweight title)*
Dec 11, 1981	**Trevor Burbick**	L10	QEII Sports Centre, Nassau, Bahamas

Total fights: 61; wins by knock out: 37; wins by decision: 19; losses by decision: 4; losses by knock out: 1.

BIBLIOGRAPHY

The Early Years

1. Thomas Hauser, *Muhammad Ali, His Life And Times*, Simon & Schuster, 1992. p.18.
2. Muhammad Ali with Richard Durham, *The Greatest*, Random House, 1976, p. 46.
3. Jack Olsen, *Black Is Best*, Putnam, 1967, p.74.
4. Hauser, p.15.
5. Ibid, p. 21.
6. Wilfrid Sheed, *Muhammad Ali*, Thomas Y. Crowell, 1974, p.57.
7. Ibid, p. 52.
8. Durham, p.34.

Olympics

1. Hauser, p.21.
2. Durham, p.83.
3. Hauser, p. 25.
4. *GQ* Magazine, April, 1998, p.234.
5. John Contrell, *Man of Destiny*, Muller Publishers, 1967, p.29.

Early Fights

1. *Boxing Illustrated*, February, 1963, p.6.
2. Ibid, p.6.
3. Hauser, p.33.
4. Ibid, p.39.
5. Ibid, p.45.
6. *Baltimore Sun*, March 9, 1963.
7. *New York Times*, November, 19, 1962.
8. Durham, p.112.

Buildup to Liston Fight

1. *New York Times*, July 23, 1963.
2. Durham, p.114.
3. Ibid. p.114.
4. Ibid, p.114.
5. Hauser, p.60.
6. Durham, p.112.
7. *New York Post*, November 6, 1963.
8. *Philadelphia Daily News*, September 30, 1963.
9. *Louisville Courier-Journal*, February 3, 1964.
10. *Harpers Magazine*, June, 1964.
11. *New York Times*, February, 26, 1964.
12. Howard Bingham, Muhammad Ali, *A Thirty-Year Journey*, Simon & Schuster, 1993.
13. Durham, p.119.
14. Ibid, p.119.

Ali Refuses Induction-Exile

1. *Sports Illustrated*, October 26, 1970.
2. Jose Torres, *Sting Like A Bee*, Abelard-Schuman, 1971, p.147.
3. *Washington Star*, February, 27, 1964.
4. *New York Post*, February 22, 1966.
5. Durham, p.143.
6. *Sports Illustrated*, May 8, 1967.
7. *Muhammad Speaks*, April 4, 1969.

Comeback vs. Quarry

1. Hauser, p.207.
2. *Baltimore Sun*, October 25, 1970.
3. Hauser, p.171.
4. Ibid, p.210.
5. Durham, p. 265.

Ali-Frazier—Fight of the Century

1. *Baltimore Sun*, March 8, 1991.
2. Ibid.
3. Ibid.
4. *New York Post*, January 14, 1971.
5. *New York Daily News*, Feb. 20, 1971.
6. *Baltimore Sun*, March 9, 1971.
7. Ibid, March 3, 1971.
8. *Baltimore Sun*, March 9, 1971.
9. Muhammad Ali with Richard Durham, *The Greatest*, p. 356.
10. *Baltimore Sun*, March 9, 1971.
11. Norman Mailer, *Life*, March 19, 1971.

The Broken Jaw

1. *San Diego Evening Tribune*, March 21, 1973.
2. *Los Angeles Times*, Sept. 2, 1973.
3. *Sports Illustrated*, June 6, 1978.
4. Muhammad Ali with Richard Durham, *The Greatest*, p.28.
5. *San Diego Evening Tribune*, March 21, 1973.
6. Dave Anderson, *In The Corner*, Morrow, p.235.
7. Thomas Hauser, *Muhammad Ali, His Life and Times*, p.252.
8. *Los Angeles Times*, Sept. 2, 1973.
9. Atyeo and Dennis, *The Holy Warrior*, p.93.
10. Durham, p.23.

Rumble in the Jungle

1. George Foreman and Joel Engel, *By George*, Villard Books, p.107.
2. *Atlanta Inquirer*, Feb. 2, 1997.
3. Wilfrid Sheed, *Muhammad Ali*, Thomas Y. Crowell Co., p.147.
4. *Atlanta Inquirer*, Feb. 2, 1997.
5. *New York Times*, Oct. 24, 1974.
6. Thomas Hauser, *Muhammad Ali, His Life and Times*, Simon & Schuster, p.276.
7. Ibid.
8. Sheed, p.152.
9. Hauser, p.278

Thrilla in Manila

1. *GQ* Magazine, April, 1998.
2. Joe Frazier and Phil Berger, *Smokin' Joe*, p.154.
3. *Newsweek*, September 28, 1975.
4. *New York Times*, September, 24, 1975.
5. Bill Hughes and Patrick King, *Come Out Writing, A Boxing Anthology*, p.54.
6. Frazier, p.165.
7. Thomas Hauser, *Muhammad Ali, His Life and Times*, p.322.
8. Frazier, p.166.
9. Hauser, p.326.

Ali-Spinks, Decline

1. *Philadelphia Inquirer*, February 10, 1978.
2. Hauser, p.350.
3. *Philadelphia Inquirer*, February 17, 1978.
4. Ibid.
5. *Chicago Tribune*, February 10, 1978.
6. *Philadelphia Inquirer*, February 17, 1978.
7. John Schulian, *Writers' Fighters*, Andrews & McMeel, p.14.
8. Hauser, p.349.
9. *Philadelphia Inquirer*, February 17, 1978.
10. *New York Post*, February 16, 1978.
11. Schulian, p.15.

Ali-Holmes, The Comeback

1. *Baltimore Sun*, October 2, 1980.
2. *Baltimore Sun*, October 1, 1980.
3. *Baltimore Sun*, October 2, 1980.
4. Ibid.
5. *Baltimore Sun*, September 20, 1980.
6. Ibid.
7. *Inside Sports*, November 1980.
8. Ibid.
9. Ibid.
10. Hauser, p.412.
11. *Baltimore Sun*, October 4, 1980.
12. Ibid.
13. *New York Daily News*, October 8, 1980.

The Legend Lives On

1. New York Times, December 13, 1981.
2. Sports Illustrated, December 15, 1989.
3. Baltimore Sun, January, 17, 1992
4. Baltimore Sun, November 22, 1984.
5. Ibid.
6. New York Times, March 7, 1999.
7. Sporting News, April 28, 1997.
8. David Remnick, King of the World, Random House, p.304.
9. Ibid, p.305.

"I would like to thank Ali intimates **Angelo Dundee** and **Tom Hauser** and the great warriors who fought him-**Joe Frazier, George Foreman** and **Ken Norton,** for their insight. Most of all, to **Ali** for his time and consistent good-nature when we had time to chat beyond the flash of cameras and TV lights."

"These kids today are missing a whole lot if they don't know about the legacy of Muhammad Ali, **because no matter what era you live in, you see very few true heroes.**"

SPIKE LEE, (from the Oscar-winning documentary, *When We Were Kings*)

The publishers would like to thank the following sources for their kind permission to reproduce the pictures in this book:

Allsport Historical Collection/Hulton-Deutsch 33t, 121b, 132

Allsport U.K. Ltd. 92, 140, 142/Jack Atley 162-3, 165/Michael Cooper 156/ Gray Mortimore 159/Steve Powell 151

Allsport USA/M. Morrison 7

Associated Press Photo 30, 31, 36, 54, 61, 65, 66-7, 73-4, 75bl, 80, 81, 84b, 85tr, 121t, 146-7, 152-3/H. B. Littell 24, 25/Joe Migon Stringer 78

Corbis/Bettmann 6, 13, 17, 20, 21, 27, 28, 25, 35, 58, 63, 69, 88, 94,95b, 95t, 100, 102, 104, 105, 107cr, 120, 125b, 126, 128-9, 138-9, 143, 145, 150/Michael Brennan 5, 130/Hulton-Deutsch Collection 3/UPI 40, 42-3, 46, 84-5c, 106l, 106-7, 112-3, 117, 124, 125t

The Courier-Journal, Louisville 11, 12/Robert Steiram 64

Hulton Getty 2, 29, 33b, 90, 136, 137t/Alan Band 40-1/Central Press 16, 38, 47b, 47t, 50b /Evening Standard Collection 51/Express 41r/Fox Photos, George Freston 50t/Keystone 9, 52, 53, 72/Arnold Sachs 131

Kazumichi Hayashi/Nippon Sports 168-9

Neil Leifer 39, 44, 49, 55, 83, 86, 87, 91, 96, 101, 103, 110, 115, 116, 119, 127, 133

PA News Photo Library 32, 93/EPA 166-7/Jean-Philippe Ksiazek 161b/John MacDougall 161t/Mike Nelson 160

Popperfoto 8, 15, 48-9, 57, 75t, 97

Topham Picturepoint 23, 37, 48, 89r, 89l, 111, 137b, 157-8, 164

Endpapers: **Hulton Getty**/R. McPhedran Express

Every effort has been made to acknowledge correctly and contact the source and/copyright holder of each picture, and Carlton Books Limited apologises for any unintentional errors or omissions which will be corrected in future editions of this book.